CW00433173

The Catholic Priest:
Answering God's Call

A Vocations Initiative by The Catenian Association

The Catenians
Strengthening family life
through friendship and faith

on behalf of the
Vocations Initiative of the Catenian Association for the
Catholic Bishops' Conference of England and Wales
and the Bishops' Conference of Scotland

The Catholic Priest: Answering God's Call
is published on behalf of the
Vocations Initiative of the Catenian Association for the
Catholic Bishops' Conference of England and Wales
and the Bishops' Conference of Scotland

by
Gabriel Communications, Landmark House,
Cheadle Hulme, Cheshire SK8 7JH.

ISBN: 978-1-904657-59-0

Cover design: Brendan Gilligan

Publication edited and designed by Rob Beswick

The publishers would like to acknowledge their sincerest appreciation to Bishop Michael Evans and Fr Paul Embery, without whose assistance the publication of this book would not have been possible.

Reproduction of the History of the Church in Scotland (Chapter 2) by kind permission of Alasdair Roberts

"God has created me to do Him some definite service... He has committed some work to me... I have my mission"
Cardinal John Henry Newman

Contents

Foreword

by the Right Reverend Archbishop of Westminster, Vincent Nichols

There is no doubt that the Church is changing. The way dioceses and parishes organise themselves, the sorts of activities that they undertake and the demands that are made on them are quite different from, say, 50 years ago. The Second Vatican Council inspired initiatives that are taking root in every aspect of the life of the Church.

And, of course, the Church must change. Change is necessary if the Church is to be relevant to the needs of the modern world. What we teach and believe about the love of God in Jesus Christ remains a constant but the way we teach must be relevant to the way in which we live.

Showing the way: Archbishop Nichols

It is very timely that this book should be revised and re-published. Its publication came as the Church closed the Year of St Paul and began the Year of the Priest. St Paul understood how different and fast-changing were the communities to which he was writing, with diverse problems and circumstances. He writes in different ways to each of them because he wanted to encourage them and say things that were relevant to their own needs.

At the heart of the life of the local church is the priest. Working with and for the people in his pastoral care he must recognise their specific needs. He must also encourage everyone to take their full place in the Church community, discovering their gifts and talents and making use of them for the greater good of the community to which they belong. The life of the priest is as diverse as the needs of those he serves.

This book gives a clear description of what priesthood is today, for the Catholic Church at the beginning of the 21st Century. It will assist any reader to understand the role of the priest and I believe that it will be a valuable resource for any young man who might want to discover what it is to be a priest or to pursue some idea that he may have a vocation.

Undoubtedly, God continues to call men to priesthood. Books like this will help those who hear the call to recognise it for what it is.

+ Vincent Nichols

The Right Reverend Archbishop of Westminster, Vincent Nichols

Introduction

by the Right Reverend Archbishop of St Andrews and Edinburgh, Keith Patrick Cardinal O'Brien

I am very happy to commend this book, *The Catholic Priest: Answering God's Call*, to all who read it.

I am aware that God calls boys and young and old men to the priesthood – having heard that call myself as a primary school pupil, as a teenager and as an undergraduate at University. I answered that call by applying in turn for Junior Seminary, then for Senior Seminary and then reapplying for Senior Seminary on finishing University.

My earlier two applications had been turned down – initially by the then Archbishop of Glasgow and then by the then Archbishop of St Andrews and Edinburgh – because of a health condition, a heart murmur, which I had at that time.

However, there is a lesson there for prospective candidates for the priesthood – be persistent in trying to answer the call of Almighty God and that same God will reward you.

I continued in my desire to be a priest, not only by my prayer but through the ongoing example of priests and by reading about the priesthood and vocations from books such as this.

Our spiritual lives at this present time must be nourished, whatever your age – and we must continue to realise the importance of God's call believing, as we do, that if there is no priest, then there is no Mass, and if there is no Mass, then there is no Church.

My God, indeed, bless all who read this book and who are trying to answer God's call.

+ Keith Patrick Cardinal O'Brien.

Keith Patrick Cardinal O'Brien
Archbishop of St Andrews and Edinburgh

Chapter

1

My Vocation as a Christian

What is a Vocation?

Many people only use the term 'vocation' to talk about priests, monks and religious sisters. But this isn't entirely correct. We do believe that these people have a vocation, but to limit vocation to these few groups of people doesn't do justice to its meaning. The word actually comes from the Latin word *'vocare'* which means 'to call'. Vocation, then, is about a call in people's lives – but whose call and in whose lives?

We believe that through the ages, God has called people to co-operate with him in his plans for the world in practical ways. Many of the stories in the Old Testament are about such individuals. In the first few lines of the Bible, in the Book of Genesis, God calls creation into existence by his Word. Throughout the Old Testament, God is continually inviting the community to be his Chosen People. When Jesus comes, he also calls people to follow him and to live the kind of life he does. So then, when we talk about vocation we are talking about the call of God.

But who is this call for? You might be surprised to hear that it is for everyone, including you. The Church community believes that God calls each and every

person into existence and that he further calls us to be members of his family.

As Christians we have a distinctive vocation to live our lives according to the Gospel and example of Christ. However, it doesn't stop there. We also believe that we are created for a purpose, are loved by God and also that we are on a journey throughout our lives towards him. That journey is full of different experiences, and like on many journeys, we have to make choices about which way to go. In that journey the choices we make affect the outcome of our lives. God does not pre-determine the journey we make; rather he gives us free will – an ability to choose one way or another. God asks that we always choose good over evil, but often there may be a variety of good choices on offer and we have to make a decision. For example, one choice many people make is a career path through a particular trade or profession.

While we have the freedom to make choices, God doesn't just leave us

"At the very heart of all our ministry as priests has to be the love of God"
Cardinal Basil Hume

completely alone. He is there in our lives, inviting us to follow the path of goodness and to live according to the teachings of Jesus his Son. He further invites us to use our lives as part of his plan for the world; to enhance creation, to bring about the Kingdom of God on earth and to lead all people to the wonderful vision of his light. What is truly amazing is that I am part of this master plan. I have a role to play. I am called to become more truly the person that God wants me to be and to use the gifts and talents I have to achieve this goal.

Over a 100 years ago, an English Cardinal, John Henry Newman made this point so well in one of his spiritual reflections. He wrote: "God has created me to do Him some definite service; He has committed some work to me which he has not committed to another. I have my mission – I may never know it in this life, but I shall be told it in the next."

Once we begin to think of our lives in a vocational sense, and realise that we are called to be someone unique and to do something special as part of God's plans, our lives should be changed by this knowledge. Many questions will rise in our minds, not least what my own personal 'definite service' is to be. The challenge facing the believer, therefore, is to discern what they are being called to be and to do. This involves prayer, reflection, knowledge, discussion and discovery. This book has been produced not only to provide information about priesthood, but also to be an aid to discernment for those who are considering if the Lord might be calling them to diocesan priesthood.

Vocation in the Scriptures

The Bible is not just a single book that records a series of events. It is a collection of different types of books, and although it records and interprets actual historical events, the books of both the Old and New Testaments are primarily concerned with God's dealings with his people.

God did not create humankind and just leave us be; instead he has continued to be involved with his creation over the ages. In the Bible we have details of some of the ways in which this has occurred. Sometimes God acts directly, on other occasions he uses angels as his messengers, but often he chose to use human individuals as part of his plans.

When he does this, he doesn't use them like a puppet-master pulling the strings, but rather invites them to actively co-operate with him. Whether all of the people whom he calls initially want to be part of those plans is a different matter!

In the scriptures people are called by God to do different things for him, and they all respond in a unique way to this call. This point is best made if we examine the stories of some of those called by God to do his work. Scripture references are included so that you can read the stories for yourself and reflect on them.

In the Old Testament

Abraham (Genesis 12:1-5)

The first thing that the Lord asks of Abraham is that he is to put aside everything that he has been used to and then he is to embark on a new way of life, which will bring great reward. It is the Lord who takes the initiative and who also promises that Abraham will be great. Abraham will not be a self-made man; it is God who will accomplish the great work. What is Abraham's response to this? The story, as recorded in the book of Genesis, portrays Abraham as a man of faith who puts his trust in God despite the risks and sacrifice involved. The element of sacrifice in the story is important - it would be a huge step for Abraham to give up all the things that he was used to such as home, family, shelter and employment. As he set off to fulfil the Lord's command he was embarking on a journey that he knew virtually nothing about; anything could have happened. Later on, Abraham is once again called to completely put trust in God when the Lord asks him to sacrifice his son (Genesis 22:1-9).

Moses (Exodus 3:1-12)

Moses is called when he goes to look at the burning bush from which God speaks to him. Although Moses does not reject God's call out of hand, he is still fearful of what he may have to do. He says to God: "Who am I to go to Pharaoh?" The Lord replies that he will be with Moses in the task ahead. Moses asks a fair question, as he is worried about his own ability to undertake God's work. The Lord's reply is that he will support Moses in the task ahead and that he should not be afraid.

In this story, God uses an ordinary everyday aspect of life to reach the man he has chosen. Although the call to Moses is mediated in a very special and direct way through God's voice, the Lord chose a simple event (the bush on fire) as the first stage of Moses' calling. Although most of the vocational stories in the Bible are quite dramatic, involving the direct intervention of God or an angel, there are those that are far less dramatic - for example St Joseph decides to take Mary home as his wife following a simple dream. Few people today would claim to have had direct audible encounters with God as part of their vocational discernment; however, many can point to a simple event that occurred in life which became a grace-filled moment of vocational discernment or a turning point. The fact that these moments may not sound as exciting as many of the vocational events related in the scriptures does not make these people's particular vocation any less real than the ones related in the Bible.

Jeremiah (Jeremiah 1:1-10)
Like Moses, Jeremiah is unsure as to why the Lord chose him to fulfil his plans. As he relates in his story, he protested to God that he was not able to be a prophet as he was not capable of doing the things a prophet does. He compares himself to a child who is unable to speak eloquently to those to whom he may be sent, but Lord reassures him, telling him not to fear as I, the Lord, will speak through you.

In the story of Jeremiah, the Lord empowers the prophet, telling him that his mission will involve both destruction and building; therefore Jeremiah is called upon to exercise prudence – it may well be that his mission will make him unpopular with some people. Jeremiah is told to remember that as a prophet he is doing God's work, not his own, and that he has a responsibility which may bring him into conflict with others. It is also the case that the prophet needs to preach not only by word, but also by deed.

Samuel (1 Samuel 3:1-21)
Clearly at the time of his calling, Samuel was a very young boy, and yet God still had a place for him in his work. Some may find it surprising that God chose someone so young and inexperienced in the ways of the world, but the fact remains that he was called. The story of Samuel reminds us that God calls very different types of people for his special work. It is not possible to put labels on them or to identify certain characteristics that are common to all whom he calls. Each has strengths and weaknesses, as well as different temperaments

and ideas. In Samuel's story the part played by Eli the priest is important. It is Eli who realises who it is that is really calling the boy and he helps him to respond to that call.

Jonah (Jonah 1:1-16)

The story of Jonah is worthy of special mention as it tells of how this man, who the Lord chose, tries to run away in the vain hope that God will go away and leave him alone. We don't know from the story exactly why it was that Jonah didn't want to be part of God's plans, but perhaps we may assume that he was quite happy doing his own thing and didn't want to be disturbed. He may even have thought that God would just choose someone else if he refused, but it didn't work out like that.

In the New Testament

The New Testament tells of the life and work of Jesus and goes on to relate the life of the early Church community. When Jesus exercised his ministry, he did not do so in isolation. Various people were called to co-operate with the work he was to accomplish. Firstly Mary was called by God to be the virgin mother of Jesus; Joseph was called to be Jesus' foster-father. When he started teaching and preaching, Jesus surrounded himself with the 12 apostles whom he specially called to help him – not only as assistants but as real workers. He entrusted to the apostles the task of carrying on his work after he had returned to his Father.

Mary: (Luke 1:26-38)

The story of the Annunciation is well known to us. It is a story of faith and trust in God by a young girl whom he calls for a unique task - that of giving birth to Jesus, who enters into time and space as true God and true man. The angel, who is charged with the mission of announcing God's plans to Mary, greets her with the words "Rejoice, so highly favoured". The first thing that we can learn from this story, then, is that it is a great privilege to be chosen by God to serve him in a special way.

And what is Mary's response? St Luke tells us that she was disturbed by the angel's words and wonders why she has been chosen, but the angel reassures her that this is God's will and she has nothing to fear. "I am the handmaid of the Lord," replies Mary, "let what you have said be done to me." Despite the responsibilities, consequences and difficulties that will come her way as a result of saying "Yes" to God, Mary accepts what he has in mind for her because she knows that she is called to serve the Lord in complete trust and selflessness.

St Luke is our primary scriptural source for information about Our Lord's early years and the part that Mary plays in God's plan of salvation. It is St Luke who portrays Mary as the perfect disciple, who actively co-operates with God in every aspect of her life. It is the generosity of her response that comes over so clearly when we read the gospel stories.

> "According to Saints Luke, Matthew and Mark, the first apostle to be called is Peter the fisherman...Peter is an ordinary man with an ordinary job and yet he is chosen by Jesus as leader of the apostles"

Peter (Luke 5:1-11)

According to Saints Luke, Matthew and Mark, the first apostle to be called is Peter the fisherman. Peter is not a 'professional' religious person, just an ordinary man with an ordinary job and yet he is chosen by Jesus as leader of the apostles. If we look elsewhere in the gospels we find that he is quite a character, with clear personality traits. In his favour, he is willing to try something new, he is a man who makes quick decisions, is not afraid to speak his mind, but he can also be a very humble man. We must also consider the fact that he can be impetuous, scared and, at times, out of his depth. Perhaps if we were to look for a perfect model of an individual's response to God's call, Peter might not be at the top of the list, but he teaches us that there is nothing special about the people God calls: they are ordinary people from ordinary backgrounds but, with the help of the Lord, they do extraordinary things.

It is also to Peter's credit that he is able to change his life for the Lord on the basis of a simple invitation. He doesn't need lots of time to weigh up the pros and cons – the invitation of Jesus alone is enough to make him drop everything. He changes from being a fisherman to a fisher-of-men. The step he made is similar to the one that Abraham made, namely that both were willing to give up the security of their old lifestyles for the sake of doing God's will when he called them.

Peter's humility is not always at first self-evident. It is easy to see him as someone who is, well, not so much proud but who doesn't always look before he leaps, and then finds himself the centre of attention. But that is too simplistic a view, and we have to balance that with the fact that when Peter experiences the power of God, (for example when he has tried, and failed, to walk on the water) he realises that he is not so important after all when compared to the Lord who has called him; he is soon on his knees recognising his unworthiness for so great a calling.

The Rich Young Man (Mark 10:17-22)

Possibly this is one of the saddest stories in the gospels. It must have grieved Jesus that one in whom he saw such potential could not take the step of following him. The young man (whose name we do not know) appears to have been one of those people who had done everything right so far. He kept the

Servant to the Church: His Holiness
Pope Benedict XVI blesses a newly
ordained priest in the Vatican

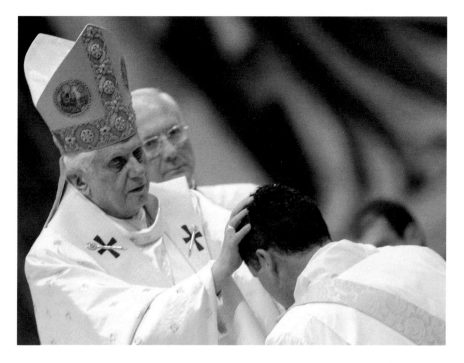

Law and was clearly dedicated to God. Without sounding too proud, he could claim that he had kept all the main commandments since his earliest days. Here was someone whose personality and lifestyle made him an attractive character. In relating the story, St Mark tells us that "Jesus loved him" and was obviously keen to have him as one of his close followers. And yet he walks away because he cannot give up his riches for the sake of following Jesus.

Possibly Jesus found his weak spot. Although he claimed to have a deep love of God, and probably did, he felt that he could not give away the riches that meant a great deal to him. This story illustrates very clearly the sacrifices that many of those whom God calls have to make. Jesus calls the young man to absolute poverty; he asks him to sell all his possessions and give the money to the poor. Today, the Church does not call priests to the same absolute poverty; however, they are asked to try to adopt a lifestyle that is an alternative to that of the people around them.

Paul (Acts 9:1-9)

The conversion of St Paul was an event of great significance for the early Church, not least because he had been a most ardent persecutor of Christians. In fact he clearly felt this to be a holy duty. Not only was he a proud man, but also clearly he was not someone who was open to the opinions and beliefs of others. He was, quite literally, blindly going down a road which was consuming him with anger and bitterness. It took the dramatic intervention of God to change this. After this special and unusual encounter, Paul is a completely different person and became a keen preacher of Jesus and the Gospel message. Perhaps the supreme irony of Paul's life was that, until he encountered Jesus on the road to Damascus, he had believed he was working for God, when in reality he had, in fact, been working against him. Paul had made up his mind and set out to apply his ideas without ever stopping to ask himself whether he was right or not.

Vocation and the Saints

Nearly every date throughout the year is associated with one or more saints. A saint is an individual whose example of Christian living makes them a model worthy of imitation. What constitutes sainthood varies. Some are martyrs, some teachers, some single, some married. What the saints have in common is that other people recognised something in them which made them different

– usually they powerfully demonstrated their love of God and others by the way they lived their lives.

Since the earliest days of the Church, individuals have been identified and declared saints by the Church, often after local acclaim. This practice continues to the present day – for example, Mother Teresa of Calcutta and Pope John Paul II have both been widely praised for their examples of Christian living. It is possible that one or both of them may be declared saints in the future.

One thing that is common to saints is that they did God's will and followed their individual vocations. For St Therese of Lisieux, this involved living as a Carmelite nun in a life of prayer and quiet devotion. For St Edmund Campion it involved a radical life-change and cruel martyrdom in bearing witness for Christ.

Although many of the stories of the lives of the saints are surrounded by significant events, even mystical happenings, it is often simply their determination to live a holy life, having discerned God's will, that makes them memorable.

St John Vianney, for example, was working as a farm hand and felt a call to priesthood when he was 18 years old. Despite having only the most rudimentary of educations, he pursued his vocation, even though he struggled at every stage. No one expected anything particularly special of him, and several years after his ordination he was sent to a small and fairly neglected poor parish in Ars, France. Over the following decades his preaching and example transformed the village, so much so that thousands of people travelled to listen to him and receive the sacrament of reconciliation. He often found himself spending up to sixteen hours a day in the confessional as well as delivering a daily sermon.

Another saint, Elizabeth of Hungary, was an altogether very different character. Born into a royal family, Elizabeth was destined for a luxurious and privileged life. She married at the age of 14 and had several children. However, far from revelling in court life, Elizabeth chose to dedicate much of her time to helping those less fortunate. She established a hospital for the poor near to the royal castle and worked in this herself. She also took in orphans, which she provided for from her own estate. Following the death of her husband and the intrigue that followed, Elizabeth fell on difficult times. She chose to renounce

"Every Christian shares in the call to holiness...all of the baptised are called to sanctity in their daily circumstances, whatever these may be"

the world and took the habit of a Franciscan Tertiary, working again with the poor and destitute. She even turned down the offer of a nobleman to take care of her. She died, aged only 23.

It is important to remember that it is not only a few who are called to sainthood – every Christian shares in the universal call to holiness, a point reiterated at the Second Vatican Council. All of the baptised are called to sanctity in their daily life circumstances, whatever these may be. A married couple is called to holiness no less than the Pope. Sanctity is achieved by ordinary people living out their vocations in heroic ways. No doubt there are many unsung saints who have not even been noticed, but all of us are called to follow Christ as best we can. A saint is not necessarily one who has lived their vocation perfectly, but perhaps one who recognises their imperfections as they live it out, knowing that they can rely on the grace and mercy of Almighty God.

Vocation at the Heart of Christian Life

Throughout history, the Church's understanding and theology of vocation has undergone significant change, and it would certainly be unfair to claim that a single, unified, teaching has always been universally held. Various saints and writers give us glimpses of their own personal thoughts and reflections on the matter – these often reflect the prevailing climate in the Church at the time.

During the 15th and 16th centuries, the personal and individual vocation of the Christian became one of the points of theological debate. Martin Luther (1483-1546), one of the leading protestant thinkers, developed personal vocation as a key part of his theology. "Everyone must tend his own vocation and work" is one of Luther's famous quotes.

Given the social and political upheaval in Europe at that time and the attacks on the Catholic Church, not surprisingly there was an unwillingness to embrace the ideas of the Protestants. Nevertheless, there was not a rejection of the theology of personal vocation. St Ignatius Loyola (1491-1556), the founder of the Jesuits, writes about the individual's personal vocation in his Spiritual Exercises. In this work he refers to Christ, the eternal king, directing his summons not only to "all", but "to each one in particular". In a section entitled *Intro-duction to Making a Choice of a Way of Life*, St Ignatius warns against assuming priesthood is better than marriage (or vice versa). He is also keen to stress that our choices in life should be determined after we have discerned the will and plan of God for us, not the other way round [*Spiritual Exercises* n169].

By the end of the 19th Century, well before the Second Vatican Council of the 1960's, the theology of personal vocation began to develop further. In England, John Henry Newman was writing about the subject even before he became a Catholic. In the United States, the Benedictine, Dom Virgil Michel approached it from the perspective of the Liturgical Revival and a movement known as Catholic Action. In his writings, Dom Virgil promotes the reform of the liturgy, asking for far more lay involvement in the Mass. He links this to St Paul's teaching about the Body of Christ in his First Letter to the Corinthians.

Catholic Action was a movement which was particularly strong in the early part of the 20th Century. It sought to encourage lay Catholics to put the Church's social teaching into practice in the world, especially in the circumstances of their individual daily lives. However, Catholic Action defined this work as lay participation in the apostolate of the Hierarchy; that is to say, lay people were doing something to assist the bishops and priests in their work. Catholic Action did not particularly see lay people as having their own distinctive apostolate. However, despite this limited vision, Catholic Action played an important role in its time and also marked a real development in the Church's thinking about the laity.

During the Second Vatican Council the theme of the common vocation of all the baptised appears in a number of the major documents of the Council. In the document on the Church, *Lumen Gentium* paragraph 11 says of parents looking after their children, "they must foster the vocation that is proper to each of them". Even the document devoted to the life of priests emphasises that it is part of a priest's work to ensure that "each member of the faithful shall be led in the Holy Sprit to the full development of his own vocation in accordance with the Gospel teaching, and to sincere and active charity, and the liberty with which Christ has set us free".

"For the whole community of the People of God and for each member of it what is in question is not just a specific social membership; rather, for each and every one what is essential is a particular vocation"
Pope John Paul II

During his pontificate, Pope John Paul II often spoke about personal vocation. In his first encyclical *Redemptor Hominis* of March 1979 he wrote: "For the whole community of the People of God and for each member of it what is in question is not just a specific social membership; rather, for each and every one what is essential is a particular vocation" (n21). This theme is poignantly re-echoed in his 1985 apostolic letter to the youth of the world, *Dilecti Amici,* in which the Pope spelled out the development in vocational thinking that has followed the Second Vatican Council. He said: "The Council has broadened this way of looking at things. Priestly and religious vocations have kept their particular character and their sacramental and charismatic importance in the life of the People of God. But at the same time the awareness renewed by the Second Vatican Council of the universal sharing of all the baptised in Christ's three-fold prophetic, priestly and kingly mission... have led to a realisation of the fact that every human life vocation, as a Christian vocation, corresponds to an evangelical call".

In 1997, delegates from all over Europe (including Eastern Europe) met in Rome for a congress devoted to vocations to the priesthood and religious life. The final report from the congress, *In Verbo Tuo* uses the terminology of personal vocation throughout. In fact the congress proved to be a seminal moment in our current way of thinking about vocation in England and Wales. The message that came out of the congress, loud and clear, is that the best way to promote vocations to priesthood and religious life isn't in isolation or simply by periodic initiatives or advertising campaigns, but by creating a whole culture of vocation in the Church. If the Church really stresses the vocation that all have through baptism then, from this vision, particular vocations, including priesthood, will flow. To quote one section of *In Verbo Tuo*: "If at one time vocations promotion referred only or mainly to certain vocations, now it must tend ever more towards the promotion of all vocations, because, in the Lord's Church, either we grow together or no one grows".

It is important to realise that in the Vatican II understanding of Church and vocation, there is a hierarchy in the Church, but not a hierarchy of vocations. That is to say, while we may respect and listen to a bishop because of his office, we shouldn't view other people as being more or less important because of their particular vocation. In God's eyes, we are all important and each of us receives a mission, a vocation, to preach the Good News of God's Kingdom.

Am I Called to Priesthood?

You may be reading this book for one of several reasons. You might be a school pupil researching for a Religious Education project, or possibly you just came across the book and thought it might be interesting. However, it might also be the case that you are reading it because you are interested in the priesthood. As has already been said, given that we all have a vocation in life, it is important that we spend time trying to discern what it might be. One option that Catholic young men should at least give some thought to is whether their particular vocation might be to serve as a priest. Many of them will instantly, almost like an involuntary reflex, say that it isn't for me. That may well be the case, but it should only be viewed as such after giving priesthood serious thought and reflection. Often it can be dismissed out of hand simply because it seems a big challenge, or because of a misunderstanding about what a priest really is and what he does. This book spells out in fairly simple terms what it means to be a priest, but it is not the final word on the matter. Hopefully, after reading it, you will have a greater understanding of the priesthood, and if it is something that you are considering, you will be better equipped to discern the call of God in your life.

One thing that we can be certain about is that the Church does need priests. The priesthood has always been a fundamental part of the life of the Church, not just in worship, but also in leadership of the local community. The Second Vatican Council reminded us that priests have a chief role to play in the renewal of the Church. The more that lay people become actively involved in the life and mission of the Church, the more the priest is needed to sustain and empower them for service of the Lord.

The call to priesthood is similar to that of the apostles. They stayed close to Jesus, but were also close to the people they were called to lead. Jesus is still with the Church today. Through the power of the Holy Spirit he is present in the sacraments, in his living Word, and also through the ministry of those who are called to ordained service. Through bishops, priests and deacons, Jesus continues his own ministry of the Good Shepherd, Teacher and High Priest of his Church. That is why the priesthood remains, and will always be, so vital to the Church's life and work.

Could I be amongst those being called today by God to this ministry? This is certainly a question for any young Catholic man, who fulfils the Church's criteria for priesthood, to consider. Perhaps this is the first time you have asked yourself this question, or possibly you thought about it a number of years ago and it has come back to you. Maybe others have suggested the priesthood to you, and you are wondering if they could be right. It may even be the case that a priest you know has inspired you and you simply want to know more.

If at this stage you are considering priesthood and are feeling a little hesitant, don't worry, this is quite normal. The priestly ministry is a real challenge and, understandably, those who feel called to it will have their concerns as to whether they can live up to what may be being asked of them. Like so many of those called by God, you will no doubt feel inadequate or unworthy to undertake so great a role. You may feel too young or inexperienced, or may have questions about some of the sacrifices that you would be asked to make. Possibly you think that you don't have the right qualifications or just feel overwhelmed by the whole idea that it might be for you.

If any of these thoughts ring true for you, then you are in good company. Many of those whom God has called in the past – prophets of the Old Testament, the apostles and countless saints – have all felt inadequate when faced with the call of God in their lives. However, this reality only confirms that the Lord calls ordinary people to do extraordinary things for him, and that as his servants we are only the 'earthenware vessels' bearing the treasure of the living Jesus.

We are called to have faith and trust in God and to realise that we are not called because we are special, rather we are special because we are called! Like the disciples, we are challenged to "put out into the deep" (Luke Ch 5), to take a step forward on our faith journey, not quite knowing where it will lead, but doing so safe in the knowledge that God is with us and will never ask us to do anything without giving us the grace to complete the task.

> "Help me to find my true vocation in life, and grant that through it I may find happiness myself and bring happiness to others.
> Grant, Lord, that those whom you call to enter the priesthood or the religious life may have the generosity to answer your call, so that those who need your help may always find it.
> We ask this through Christ our Lord. Amen."

Chapter

Priesthood and the Church: An Overview

The Priesthood of Christ

To understand anything that the Christian community does or teaches, it is necessary to appreciate why Jesus came amongst us in the first place. God the Father sent his Son into the world for a purpose and at an allotted time. If we look at the Old Testament scriptures we read of God's plans. He is the creator of all things. He creates man and woman and gives them a unique place in all that he has made; and yet humankind turns from him in sin. From this moment, God begins his plan to save humankind from the effects of sin. God picks a Chosen People and enters into a series of special relationships with them (known as 'covenants'); and yet his people let him down time and time again.

Eucharistic Prayer 4 in the Mass speaks eloquently about this:
"You formed us in your own likeness and set us over the whole world to serve you. Even when we disobeyed you and lost your friendship, you did not abandon us to the power of death, but helped all people to seek and find you. Again and again you offered a covenant to us and through the prophets taught us to hope for salvation. Father, you so loved the world that in the fullness of time you sent your only Son to be our saviour..."

It is in this role as Saviour that we must consider the priesthood of Christ. As Saviour, Christ restores the relationship that humankind once had with God. By his death and resurrection, eternal life is offered to all. His self-offering on the cross for the forgiveness of sin supersedes all the sacrifices of the Old Testament. At the last supper Jesus said, "This is the cup of my blood, the blood of the new and everlasting covenant; it will be shed for you and for all so that sins may be forgiven". On the altar of the cross, Christ, the priest, offers himself in sacrifice to the Father.

The day on which this sacrifice took place is now called Good Friday. It is rightly called 'good' because of what Jesus did for us. It shows the love that God has for us all. In his letters, St John tells us that God is love (1 John 4:8), and in the gospel of St John we hear that God loved the world so much that he sent his only Son (John 3:16). It is not that God demonstrates just a kind of love; rather that God is love. He loves us completely, totally, unreservedly and unconditionally. This is truly good news and is at the heart of the gospel message. In fact, the word 'gospel' that we use today is based on the Anglo-Saxon 'god-spell' which means good tidings. Throughout the gospels, the story of all that Jesus said and did is, above all, a story of love. That love is shown most powerfully when Jesus laid down his life in sacrifice. "A man can have no greater love than to lay down his life for his friends" (John 15:13).

The priest today is called to be 'like Christ'. He is to make present once again Christ's sacrifice through celebration of Mass. He is to be a minister of good news to the people he serves so that the liberating message of the gospel will affect every area of their lives and also the life of the wider community. He is to be a minister of joy and a visible sign of God's love; and not just a sign, but a means by which the love of God is demonstrated in a real way in the lives of others, especially those in need. He will also be called to lay down aspects of his own life in imitation of Christ.

Clearly, to be an effective minister of God's love and a shepherd to the people, the priest must love not only Christ, but also his Church. The Church is not simply an institution or building; rather it is the living Body of Christ – it is the People of God. The role of the priest is to lead that people and to be like Christ to them. In imitation of his master, the priest must remember that this is a leadership of service. Christ said that he came not to be served, but to serve (Matthew 20:28). The role of the priest is to minister to the members who make

Picture above is of a steel engraving of Christ, made in Germany, date unknown

"The priest today is called to be 'like Christ'. He is to make present once again Christ's sacrifice through celebration of Mass. He is to be a minister of good news to the people he serves..."

up the Church and who carry out its mission in the circumstances of their daily lives, according to their vocation and the gifts they have been given. In order to do this effectively he must have a genuine concern and love for them, remembering that while he has been called to a ministry of leadership in the community, he still remains very much a member of it. Like the Good Shepherd, he should have a great love for the sheep (John 10).

The risen Christ remains Lord of his Church. He is the only Head of the Church, with all those who lead the Church in his name sharing in his authority. Any ministries in the Church are signs and instruments of the risen Lord present and active amongst us. Without him we can do nothing (John 15:5). The Catechism of the Catholic Church (CCC), quoting St Thomas Aquinas, makes it clear that only Christ is the true priest, the others being only his ministers (CCC 1545).

At the heart of the Catholic faith is the gift of 'sacrament', with the invisible presence of Christ made powerfully present through something visible. For example, in the pouring of the water of baptism Christ is made present in the life of the new Christian.

The Second Vatican Council teaches us that the word 'sacrament' isn't limited to the seven sacramental actions of the Church, namely: Baptism, Eucharist, Confirmation, Ordination, Marriage, Reconciliation and the Sacrament of the Sick. *Lumen Gentium*, one of the documents of the Council, teaches us that the Church itself is a sacrament, a visible sign of Christ's presence and power. We all share in that sacramental life, configured as we are to Christ, and he works through all of us, uniting his Church and continuing his saving work. Therefore the role of all the baptised in Christ's Body, the Church, needs to be continually stressed and developed, but there is also something special about the priest's role in relation to Christ's sacramental ways of acting. It is in the administration of the sacraments that the role of the ordained priest is so unique and important. This will be explained in more detail later in this book.

At his ordination, a priest becomes a co-worker with his bishop. Everything a priest does flows from what he becomes at his ordination. Therefore, we cannot primarily define a priest by the jobs he does; *it is what he is* that matters first and foremost. The priest does what he does because of what he is: a priest of Jesus Christ. To fully understand this, it is important to have some knowledge of how the priesthood has developed in the Church over time.

The Apostles and Early Church

All those who believed in Jesus were called to follow him, but he chose from amongst them a small group of men to work with him more closely. It would later be these men, the apostles, who would lead the early Church and continue the work of Jesus.

Being an apostle involved a sense of being called. Jesus said to the Twelve: "You did not choose me, but I chose you" (John 15:16), and Saint Paul was very conscious of being "set apart for the Gospel of God" (Romans 1:1). There was always therefore, a group within the larger community of believers who were called to dedicate themselves to Jesus and his ministry in a permanent and special way.

To be an apostle was to be someone with Jesus and to be someone sent by Jesus. Being with Jesus is about witness. In the early days of the Church, it was important that Christ's words and actions were accurately recalled so that the Gospel could be proclaimed. The apostles were able to do this because they had been witnesses of all that Jesus said and did and particularly of his resurrection. Eventually, the words and actions of Jesus were written down in the four gospels we know today.

Being sent by Jesus means proclaiming the Good News to the world. He commanded his apostles "Go therefore and make disciples of all nations" (Matthew 28:19). This proclamation ensures that the story of Jesus and God's plan of salvation are shared with people throughout the world and down the centuries.

In the Creed, which is recited by the community at each Sunday Mass, we profess our belief in a Church that is "one, holy, catholic and apostolic". By apostolic we mean that it is based on the teaching and tradition of the apostles, who were commissioned by Christ to continue his work. One of the hallmarks of unity and fellowship in the Church is our link to the apostles. Catholic tradition also affirms that the ordained ministry provides an unbroken link to Jesus through the apostolic line, thus guaranteeing that we are truly part of his Body, the Church.

The writings of St Paul in the New Testament provide us with a valuable insight as to how he saw the role of apostle or someone who shared the ministry of the apostles. St Paul sees himself as a servant of the Gospel (Ephesians 3:7), of the Church (Colossians 1:25) and of Christ Jesus (Philippians 1:1). In the First Letter to the Corinthians he describes himself as a fellow-worker with God, the slave of everyone and as steward of the mysteries of God. In the Second Letter to the Corinthians he is an envoy, ambassador and servant of reconciliation.

He can serve the Church in these capacities because of the authority he has received from the Lord (2 Corinthians 10:8). In the Letter to the Romans (15:16), he describes himself as a priest of Jesus Christ, and carrying out his priestly duty in order that the pagans may be made an acceptable offering to God. In his later letters, notably to Timothy and Titus, Paul talks about the qualities of leadership in the community. In these he makes mention of 'elders' (in Greek, *presbyteros*) and the ministry of 'overseer' (*episcopos*).

In the New Testament Letter to the Hebrews, the author explains the priesthood of Christ, particularly in its relationship to the priesthood of the Old Testament, which is fulfilled by Christ's sacrificial death on the cross. That Christ is now the one, eternal priest (Hebrews 7:24) is at the heart of the Church's understanding and theology of the priestly ministry today.

We know from the Letter to the Ephesians that there were different types of leadership roles in the Church, including 'apostles, prophets, evangelists, pastors and teachers' (Ephesians 4:11-12). Whatever names were given to various roles in different places, a ministry of pastoral oversight for leading and uniting the communities founded by the apostles was present in the Early Church. This ministry of oversight varied according to the needs and circumstances of particular communities, so we should not expect to find any uniform pattern of leadership in the Church's early years. The New Testament says virtually nothing about who actually celebrated the Eucharist in the early Church communities; however the fact that it was central to Christian life and worship and has been handed down over the centuries, would suggest that the apostles were faithful to Jesus' command "Do this in memory of me".

By AD 100, there is widespread evidence of a style of leadership based on a model of presbyter-bishop. In the letters of St Ignatius of Antioch (AD 107) the bishop is seen as distinctive from his presbyters and deacons. By AD 200 this model had largely been adopted throughout the Church, with each grade of this three-fold ministry being received through prayer and the laying-on of hands. When the bishop was unable to be present, his presbyters deputised for him in their local communities, similar to priests today.

Theology of Priesthood Today

As the Church evolved over the years, the roles of bishop, priest and deacon

Picture courtesy of JOHN ROSS

also developed. Once Christians were free to worship in the Roman Empire without persecution, ordained ministers became more public. Eventually, Christianity became the official religion of the Empire in its latter years and was generally adopted throughout Europe.

In parallel, the Church also started to become a major player in public life. In some places, bishops became civil as well as religious leaders. The Pope, too, assumed a temporal as well as spiritual role and had his own kingdom which covered much of what is now central Italy. Educated clergy took leading jobs in newly emerging nation states; for example in England, Thomas Becket, Archbishop of Canterbury, was also Chancellor for the King.

Medieval theology developed the idea of ordination as one of the seven sacraments and, notably, that like Baptism and Confirmation, ordination effected a 'character' change in the man receiving it. He is literally a 'marked man', set aside permanently and irrevocably by Christ. During the middle and late 16th Century, thinkers such as Luther and Calvin felt that the Church was in need of reform. One area that they concentrated on was the priesthood, the significance of which, they felt, had been overstressed. They put more emphasis on the role and vocation of lay people. As part of their understanding of justification by faith alone, they initially rejected the need for ordained ministers as 'intermediaries' between God and his People, but later came to accept that they were necessary although in a very different way from the Catholic understanding of the priesthood.

At the Council of Trent (1545-63), the Catholic Church affirmed the medieval understanding of ordination as one of the seven sacraments. The priesthood is not just about preaching the gospel, but includes the power of consecrating and offering the Body and Blood of Christ at the Eucharistic Sacrifice, as well as the forgiveness of sins. Understandably, given the attacks on the Church, Trent reaffirmed many of the cultic aspects of the priesthood, emphasising its distinctiveness in the life of the Church. This teaching, although never considered as the final word on the priesthood, was to dominate Church thinking for several centuries. More recently, insights gained from new study of the scriptures and other Church writings, and also ecumenical discussions, have opened the way for a fuller and richer understanding of priesthood.

The Second Vatican Council stressed the vocation of every Christian to be active in the life and mission of the Church. The whole people are called to minister, to serve and to live out their priestly vocation given to them in baptism. Nevertheless, to do this, they need ordained priests, who are Christ's own living instruments for building up his Church.

The Council did not change the Church's teaching on the priesthood, rather it developed or enhanced it by setting it in the context of the dignity and responsibility of all the members of Christ's body. Whilst affirming the traditional teaching about the cultic role of the priest, the Council also encouraged fresh thinking about what it means to be a priest, with more emphasis being given to the roles of being a witness, a servant and a shepherd.

The 'Decree on the Priestly Life and Ministry' (*Presbyterorum Ordinis*) sums up the Council's understanding and teaching about the priesthood. It sees the priest as participating in the office of the apostles, and being a co-worker with the bishops. But even more than that, the decree says "the priest shares in the authority by which Christ himself builds up, sanctifies and rules his body", and indeed that priests are "so configured to Christ, the priest, that they can act in the person of Christ the Head" (P.O. 2).

Lord Jesus
I give you my hands
To do your work
I give you my feet
To go your way.
I give you my eyes
To see as you do.
I give you my tongue
To speak your words.
I give you my mind
That you may think in me.
I give you my spirit
That you may pray in me.
Above all, I give you my heart
That you may love in me your Father and all humanity.
I give you my whole self that you may grow in me,
So it is you, Lord Jesus
Who live and work and pray in me

Grail prayer

This is not about putting the priest between Christ and his People; rather the priest is the sign and instrument of Christ's direct and immediate leadership of the faithful. By their calling priests are in a real sense 'set apart', but this is done within the context of being in the midst of Christ's People. The setting apart does not remove priests from the people but enables them to be dedicated to the Lord's work.

The Catechism of the Catholic Church teaches, in accordance with what was said at the Second Vatican Council, that the priesthood is ministerial, ie, a service (CCC 1551). It also reminds us that although the priest is set apart and that Christ is present in him as an ordained minister; however, this is not to be understood to mean that he is preserved from human weakness, error or sin. (CCC. 1550).

In 1992, Pope John Paul II issued an exhortation to the Church regarding the formation of future priests 'Pastores Dabo Vobis' ('I will give you shepherds'). In this, he reiterated much of the traditional teaching of the Church regarding the ministerial priesthood, but he also states that the priest must be a man who is

"Celtic missionaries from the island of Iona re-introduced Christianity in the north of England..."

able to engage with the modern world. So we need to recognise that some aspects of the priesthood never change, while the actual way that the priestly ministry is lived out varies according to time, place and circumstance. Pope John Paul also stressed that while the priesthood is universal in the sense that it is a sharing in the universal priesthood of Christ, it is also 'particular' in that a priest is a co-worker with his bishop, called to serve the local Church.

The History of the Church In England and Wales

The Christian faith almost certainly reached England during the period of the Roman conquest. The first known martyr in England, St Alban, lived here in the third century. However, due to a succession of barbarian invasions, it was not possible to firmly establish the faith until several centuries later.

Celtic missionaries from the island of Iona re-introduced Christianity in the north of England, and in 596 Pope Saint Gregory the Great sent Benedictine monks, led by St Augustine, to preach the gospel to the kingdom of Kent. Although both groups of missionaries shared the same faith, there was some difference in liturgical practice, most notably in the liturgical calendar. At the

Synod of Whitby in 664, it was agreed that the Roman, rather than Celtic, tradition would be followed.

Four years later, St Theodore was appointed Archbishop of Canterbury by the Pope. He consolidated Christian life in the country and helped establish monastic life and schools here. However, Danish invasions in later centuries destroyed much of what had been built.

Saxon rule returned again in 1042 with King (St) Edward the Confessor, whose tomb is in Westminster Abbey in London. This, however, was short-lived, and in 1066 the Normans conquered England. Saxon bishops and abbots were gradually replaced by Norman ones and the architectural style of new church buildings also changed. Many of the great cathedrals in England date from this time, including Durham, Ely, Gloucester and Tewksbury.

Although the Church was by now firmly established in the life of the nation, with many clerics also helping with the governance of the country, this was not without the occasional conflict between ecclesiastical and secular powers. King Henry II and St Thomas of Canterbury clashed on several occasions, which ultimately led to the archbishop's martyrdom.

In the 16th Century, the whole fabric of society underwent dramatic changes. The old medieval feudal system began to collapse. Nation states were in ascendance and there was turmoil in political, social and religious life. Religious thinkers in various parts of Europe began to question the authority, teaching and practice of the Church and called for reform.

In most states where Protestantism was accepted, this was rarely done for totally religious reasons; other cultural and political factors often played a role. In England and Wales this was particularly the case, with King Henry VIII declaring himself 'Supreme Head of the Church in England'. Ironically, a few years before this, the Pope had given Henry the title 'Defender of the Faith' for his work defending the seven sacraments against the teachings of Martin Luther.

Not everyone, however, bowed to the pressure that Henry put on them to accept him as Head of the Church. The Lord Chancellor, Sir Thomas More and Bishop John Fisher of Rochester both objected to it. Both were arrested and executed for treason, though without a doubt they were martyred because they upheld the authority of the Pope.

Despite the break with Rome, many scholars argue that Henry never really embraced Protestant teaching. Although the king suppressed the monasteries and other ecclesiastical foundations, with the proceeds going to the Crown, in other respects many of the practices and customs of the Church were retained. It was only with the accession of the young Edward VI in 1547 that England moved towards Protestantism.

In 1558 Elizabeth I came to the throne. By an Act of Parliament, it was ruled that Sunday attendance at the local parish church was compulsory. In effect this meant that it was no longer possible to attend Catholic Mass, or even to make a conscientious objection and absent oneself from the service. It is possible that at this stage Elizabeth thought that Catholicism would simply die out after a decade or so when people had got used to the new practices of religion; however, if this was her hope, it was not to be the case.

William Allen, later Cardinal Allen, was one of many Catholics who wanted to see Catholicism survive. As it was now impossible to train men for the priesthood at home due to persecution, he founded a priests' training college in Douai in 1568 with the intention of providing Catholic clergy for those who remained faithful in England and Wales. Even today, the Catholic community still has some seminaries abroad which were founded during these centuries of persecution.

In 1570 news came that Pope Pius V had excommunicated Elizabeth, thus releasing her Catholic subjects from allegiance to her. This led to even more repressive legislation against Catholics. However, despite persecution, many Catholics remained politically loyal to their country and to the Queen. In conscience they were still faithful to both to Rome and the Mass, but they could not bring themselves to rebel against the monarch. Significantly, in 1588 when the Spanish Armada arrived off the coast of England, there was no Catholic uprising; indeed, many fought to defend their country.

However, despite this show of loyalty, many Catholics still suffered for their faith. Between July 22nd and November 27th 1588, 21 priests, 11 laymen and one woman were put to death for their Catholic beliefs. In total, during

Cardinal William Allen founded the priests' training college in Douai, the first seminary overseas for the training of priests in England and Wales

Elizabeth's reign, nearly 200 Catholics were executed. Of these, over half were priests. There were also others who were not executed, but who died of starvation and the like while in custody. Many of those executed have been canonised as martyrs.

At the start of the reign of King James I in 1603, it is estimated that there were well over 300 priests operating in England and Wales, the majority of whom had been trained in the new seminaries on the continent. As a response to this, James passed a law forbidding Catholics sending their children abroad to be educated. To raise money for the Crown he also heavily fined Catholics who attended Mass. In 1605 a number of Catholic sympathisers attempted to blow up the King and Parliament in the Gunpowder Plot – an act which did little to help the Catholic cause.

"However, despite this show of loyalty, many Catholics still suffered for their faith... between July 22nd and November 27th 1588, 21 priests, 11 laymen and one woman were put to death for their Catholic beliefs... many of those executed have been canonised as martyrs"

During the reigns of subsequent monarchs life became progressively more tolerable for Catholics; however, it was not until 1829 that they were fully allowed to practise their religion. In 1850 the Hierarchy was restored in England and Wales; this meant that Catholic bishops and dioceses could be formally re-established. A large influx of Irish immigrants to the country in the 1840s and 50s further boosted the number the Catholics. Today it is estimated that there are some four million Catholics in England and Wales.

The History of the Church in Scotland

Scotland was also evangelised by Celtic missionaries who made the island of Iona their base. They moved among kinsmen who had earlier crossed from Ulster to settle in western coastal areas. Colum Cille (otherwise known as St Columba) was the first abbot of Iona.

Most journeys were by coracle on water and his own furthest one reached as far as the top of Loch Ness, where a Pictish king was given the message of Christ. Centuries later Scotland became a strongly Protestant country, and its historians regularly portrayed the wandering Celtic monks as independent of Roman authority. This was based on an appeal (couched in seemingly hostile terms) to Pope Gregory the Great for a decision on the dating of Easter. Obviously such an appeal implied communion with Rome.

The Dark Ages are so-called because most of the documents from which history is made were destroyed (mainly by Vikings) but Celtic crosses and other evidence in stone testify to the orthodox Eucharistic practice of these days. In the eleventh century a Scottish king married the English woman who was to be canonised as St Margaret. She entered into discussions with the country's religious leaders and these led to a more recognisably Roman Church as it was developing throughout Europe. Monks accepted the Benedictine rule, an abbey was built at the royal capital Dunfermline, and St Andrews became a pilgrimage centre.

The medieval *Ecclesia Scoticana* was hierarchical in the same way as the new feudal system, and under Queen Margaret's sons bishops were appointed and religious communities founded. Cathedrals rose and parishes, many with new places of worship, were defined. The Archbishop of York's claims to spiritual

St Ninian's, Tynet, 1755
by PF Anson, 'Underground Catholics in Scotland, 1622-1878'

jurisdiction north of Tweed ended when a papal bull described Scotland as the 'special daughter' of Rome. Weak Governments enabled England's Edward I to gain his reputation as 'Hammer of the Scots', Churchmen proving steadier in support for King Robert the Bruce than many of his barons. The 1320 Declaration of Arbroath (following Edward II's defeat at Bannockburn) was addressed to Rome. Despite the much-quoted baronial passage which begins 'We fight not for glory' it was largely a clergy affair.

Scotland's Church needed to be reformed by the sixteenth century. Bishops and abbots had become too close to government, and James IV making his illegitimate teenage son Archbishop of St Andrews was merely an extreme example of cynical behaviour by rulers. Religious practice became slack, but there was a strong political aspect (French alliance or English?) to Scotland's late and sudden Reformation. This outlawed the Mass by Parliamentary decree in three weeks of 1560. Mary Queen of Scots returned from France to find John Knox – returned from Protestant England – in the pulpit and Lords of the Congregation in arms. Harangued in Edinburgh and defeated in battle she fled south. As the Catholic claimant to Elizabeth's throne, she was imprisoned and eventually executed.

Mention of England's Queen recalls the many Catholic martyrs who went to their deaths at Tyburn and elsewhere. Scotland, by contrast, had only one recognised martyr, the Jesuit St John Ogilvie, who was hanged at Glasgow Cross in 1615.

Elizabeth's successor, James VI and I was shrewd enough to avoid the execution of priests, but his son Charles I applied the full force of law against Scots landholders who harboured them. Catholic gentry still formed a majority in the counties of Aberdeen and Banff, the Marquis of Huntly persuading his mainly Gordon followers to stay loyal to the old faith. Many bore the wounds of a victory in defence of it at Glenlivet. Jesuits came to the area in considerable numbers, but threats to their property caused many local leaders to become Episcopalian Protestants.

Meanwhile, parts of the north-west Highlands and Islands were being won back to Catholicism through the efforts of Irish Franciscans. Operating from a base on the Antrim coast, they saw themselves as the successors of Colum Cille. Vincentians and other regular priests also crossed the sea from Ireland, Gaelic language and culture making them ideal missionaries for the area. The north-east Lowlands were served by priests educated in Scots colleges abroad, mainly at Rome, Paris and Douai.

After the brief and ill-fated reign of the Catholic James II and VII, Thomas Nicolson was made Scotland's first bishop or vicar apostolic since the Reformation. He and his successor, Bishop James Gordon, made regular visitations of 'farr west' (where most Catholics lived) from Lowland Banffshire. They travelled with Gaelic-speaking translators.

'Worship in Wild Places' has been used to describe the old faith's survival in Scotland. A seminary at Scalan in Glenlivet also depended on remoteness to serve its function of preparing boys for the Scots colleges abroad, and another seminary moved around the west coast making it possible for Highland priests to serve their people. When the Scottish Mission was divided into Highland and Lowland Districts in 1728, the 'heather priest', Bishop Hugh MacDonald, was sent to Paris in order to experience normal Catholic practice. Soon after his appointment Highland and Lowland Scots clergy found themselves at odds over Jansenism. It was claimed that many of the latter (including Bishop Gordon) were influenced by this Paris-focused heresy which came close to Calvinism.

The '45 Rising in favour of the exiled Stuart dynasty proved – in religious terms at least – a welcome distraction. However, Scotland's Catholics suffered for rebellion along with other Jacobites and ended up as a still more-persecuted minority.

The late eighteenth century saw Highland District numbers reduced through emigration, but military service in Britain's French wars led to a degree of legal toleration for Scotland's Catholics in 1793. An earlier attempt to follow England provoked "No Popery" riots in Edinburgh and Glasgow. Highland areas apart, bishops and clergy mainly came from a small area near Speymouth. The Enzie was dubbed the *'papisticall country'* for its adherence to the religion protected by the Huntly Gordons. Protection continued after the last Catholic Duke died, but St Ninian's at Tynet is not only Scotland's oldest Catholic church still in use but also a symbol of penal times. This 'Banffshire Bethlehem' was built to resemble a sheep cote. In contrast, St Gregory's stands in grandeur nearby at Preshome. A sign of fuller Catholic emancipation to come, it was Britain's largest Mass centre outside the embassy chapels of London.

Irish immigration gathered pace in the following century and Scotland's Catholicism became predominantly urban, but Bishop James Kyle of the new Northern District (now the Diocese of Aberdeen) ended his days at Preshome.

Welcoming his love... and you are free to take on responsibilities, free even to give your life.

Through the Gospel, you know that young man who, searching in God for the will of his love, came to Christ with his questions. One day Jesus replied to him, "You are lacking one thing. Sell what you have, give it to the poor, then come, follow me." And the young man went away sad.

Why did he go away? Because he had many possessions. He wanted both to follow Christ and to keep his wealth. He did not have the freedom to give, out of love, even his own possessions.

It is human nature to wish to have everything. But anyone who wants everything teeters on the brink of impossibility; and nothing vast, nothing lasting can be accomplished then.

The young man in the Gospel was invited to make a choice of freedom. But so often in the presence of the call to give even one's life for love, it happens that the yes and the no clash. The yes fascinates; and at the same time that yes is frightening.

Will hesitations keep you at a standstill when confronted with eternity's yes, that yes which was already spoken by Mary? Let the day come for a resolution with no turning back. There comes a time when there is no other way out than a response of freedom, casting oneself upon God as into an abyss.

And then comes wonder. This abyss is God. It is not as abyss of darkness but a chasm radiant with the brightness of the Risen Lord.

Brother Roger of Taizé

Chapter

3

What is a Priest?

Proclaimer of the Good News

If you were to ask someone what a priest does, they would probably point to several key things: saying Mass, helping people and praying. You might add to this list leading the parish community and celebrating other sacraments. While these are all true, arguably the priest's most basic task is that of proclaiming the Good News, that is, preaching the gospel. The fact that the gospel has been preached presupposes all the other work of a priest.

Jesus himself proclaimed the Good News. The Gospels of Mark and Matthew record Jesus' first words of his public ministry as being the proclamation of the proximity of God's kingdom and the need to believe the Good News. The command of Jesus to his disciples after the resurrection was to teach all nations by proclaiming the Good News (Matthew 28:20 & Mark 16:16). So we can say that these gospels begin and end with the Good News; in fact, to be more precise, all four gospels have been recorded to proclaim the Good News.

And what is this 'Good News'? Really, the question should be 'Who is this Good News'? Although the Good News is that God loves us, this is made manifest in a person – namely Christ Jesus. He is Good News not only because he proclaims the Father's love and shows us how to live that love out, but also because by dying on the cross that love is perfected as he offers his life in sacrifice to take away our sins and opens the way for the salvation of all.

There are those who point out that the gospel message was brought to this country over a thousand years ago, that we have sent missionaries to other parts of the world, and that copies of the Bible abound in libraries, schools, hotel rooms and homes. It would appear that the Good News has already been adequately proclaimed here. But has it? Proclamation of the gospel is one thing, taking it to heart is another. Many of those in our communities certainly know of the gospel and may even have heard large sections of it, but whether they have really listened is perhaps another matter. The reality is that even the most devout follower of Christ needs to have the gospel continually proclaimed to them afresh, as it is the living Word of God that still speaks today. Arguably, in these times, the Church needs to proclaim the Good News with even greater fervour to let people really know about God and his love. The priest must be the first to acknowledge and carry out this task.

An important part of the priest's duties is not only to read the gospel in Mass or in the wider world, but also to preach about it. It is not that the gospel is insufficient or lacking, rather that it needs to be brought to people in a meaningful way, not least to draw their attention to its relevance in their daily lives and to open up the richness of its meaning.

Therefore, the homily at Mass is one of the most important parts of Christian worship and of a priest's work also. This does not mean that every priest is automatically going to be a first-class public speaker, but he should use the gifts that God has given him as best he can to tell others about the gospel message.

A Man of the Eucharist

If proclaiming the gospel is the first and foremost duty of a priest, then celebrating the Eucharist is next. Although the faithful are united in baptism to the Body of Christ, they are also united to it through the Eucharist. Sunday Mass in particular is one of the key moments in the life of the Church, and it is the priest who presides at this as he changes bread and wine into the Body and Blood of Christ.

Picture courtesy of JOHN ROSS

As such, the priest represents Christ at the Last Supper and he is therefore leader of the Eucharistic community. Archbishop Oscar Romero, who was shot while saying Mass in 1980 in El Salvador, once said: "It is as if a community were beheaded when it has no priest to celebrate Mass and Divinize all that is human". This saying really

"If proclaiming the gospel is the first and foremost duty of a priest, then celebrating the Eucharist is next"

gets to the heart of the significance of the role of the priest as one who leads the community through celebration of the Eucharist. It follows that the priest must be a man of the Eucharist. He becomes this not only by actually celebrating Mass, but by making the Eucharist the centre of his ministry and a source of daily nourishment. To make Christ present on earth in the sacrament of the Eucharist is an immeasurable privilege.

When priests take this to heart, the rest of their ministry flows from it. Many priests, and not only priests, spend time each day in prayer in front of Christ present in the Blessed Sacrament.

Washer of Feet – A Life of Service

The fact that a priest represents Christ the Head, present for His Church, doesn't mean that a priest should have an air of superiority about him, no matter how much people respect his important ministry. While the Gospels of Matthew, Mark and Luke all have an account of the institution of the Eucharist at the Last Supper, St John's Gospel concentrates instead on Jesus washing his disciples' feet, a task normally carried out by servants. It is not that St John is ignoring the importance of the Eucharist – the theme of Jesus as Bread of Life is mentioned elsewhere in his gospel – rather that he chose to emphasise the link between Eucharist and service.

It is no accident that the Last Supper and Jesus' death on the cross are linked. Not only do they take place within 24 hours of each other, but also Jesus is shown as giving his body and blood for us both as a sacrament and a sacrifice. Christ's moment of glory is also a moment of self-emptying. Christ humbled and emptied himself, even to death on a cross (Philippians 2:2-8). Just as giving the Eucharist was a sign of Jesus giving his life for us, the washing of the feet at the Last Supper is another sign of his complete gift of self as a servant.

Every Maundy Thursday, at the evening Mass, the priest re-enacts this action of Jesus. It is a powerful reminder to the whole community that the priest represents Christ the Head in service as well as in leadership. In his ministry, Jesus was one who served and cared for others. He is the fulfilment of the 'Suffering Servant' mentioned by the prophet Isaiah (Mark 10:45). The washing of the feet is also a reminder to the priest that he too exercises a gentle leadership based on service reflecting the same humility which Jesus himself showed throughout his life and particularly in his crucifixion and death.

Fisherman

Jesus told his first disciples that they would change from being fishermen to fishers-of-men; by this he meant that their new role involved a mission to others, particularly to 'catch' them for God. Of course, this does not imply a forced conversion or dragging people along unwillingly; it is simply an image that Jesus used to stress what the role of the apostles was – to bring people to God.

> Of its nature the Church is missionary and therefore it must be faithful to the command of Jesus to "Go, teach all nations."
> **Matthew 28:19**

If the priest today is to follow in the footsteps of the apostles, he too needs to be a fisherman, albeit in a changed world. In a society where the Church doesn't enjoy the status it used to in many people's minds, there can be a temptation to look inwardly and concentrate our efforts on those who already 'belong' rather than those who have little to do with the Church. There can also be the temptation to let people come to us, whether this be through the school system or simply by making the Church into an attractive community. While both of these are important, they cannot be all that the Church does. Of its nature the Church is missionary and therefore it must be faithful to the command of Jesus to "Go, teach all nations." (Matthew 28:19).

Over the centuries, the Church's missionary endeavours have often involved the exercise of real pastoral charity as an accompaniment to the proclamation of the gospel. For example, many missionaries to less developed parts of the world have established medical centres as a practical embodiment of the gospel values they proclaim. In his first major Encyclical Letter *God is Love*, Pope Benedict XVI reminded the Church that these acts of love for others should never be conditional on converting to Christ, but rather should demonstrate to others the love of God that the gospel message proclaims.

Therefore, the priest as a fisherman is not only servant to those who are members of the Church community, but also to those who are not. In following the example of Christ who cared for all, he must exercise his ministry, not just within the confines of church buildings, but also in the wider community. In this way the Gospel is proclaimed. It was St Francis of Assisi who told his followers to preach the gospel – and use words if you have to.

Shepherd

In St John's Gospel, Jesus describes himself as "The Good Shepherd who lays down his life for his sheep" (John 10:11). The difference between a good shepherd and a bad shepherd is that the former is really dedicated to looking after the sheep. He is interested in their well-being and will make sacrifices to help them.

In a post-resurrection appearance to the apostles, Jesus asks Peter if he loves him. When Peter says that he does, Jesus then adds "Feed my sheep." (John 21:17). It is clear that Jesus mandated the apostles to be the shepherds of his Church. As shepherd, the priest needs to have a healthy concern for the Lord's flock which has been entrusted to his care. Just as Jesus was willing to lay down his life for his flock, so too a man who feels called to be a priest must be aware of the sacrifices he is expected to make. He might not be called to literally lay down his life, but he will be asked to make a commitment to celibacy, to obedience, and to adopt a genuine poverty of spirit which is not just about material goods, but the loving surrender of his time and privacy in serving the flock.

> "One of the most moving moments at an ordination is when the man becoming a priest or deacon prostrates himself, lying flat on the ground"

New priests prostrate themselves during their ordination as priests (above). The above scene took place in the Vatican before Pope Benedict

Pope John Paul II's Apostolic Exhortation on the formation of priests *Pastores Dabo Vobis* takes its title from Jeremiah 3:15: "I will give you shepherds after my own heart". It is clear from this that the Pope had in mind that those aspiring to the priesthood should be formed as shepherds of the flock who really love as Christ loves. If the priest is to mirror the Good Shepherd he must lay down his life in service freely and with an undivided heart. The priest is asked to echo the words of Jesus as he offers his life as a joyful sacrifice, "No one takes it from me; I lay it down of my own free will." (John 10:18).

Like marriage, priesthood is a lifetime commitment. It calls for a radical and selfless giving of all that one is and has. At his ordination, the priest is able to say to God "I am yours." If his supreme desire and ambition is to serve God and his people then all the sacrifices asked of him begin to make sense, even if at times they seem difficult. Life-long celibacy, obedience and poverty come to be seen as powerful ways of living-out the commitment to be close to Christ with an undivided heart like his. This a real challenge for the priest who freely gives his all to the task of being an ambassador for Christ. It is, above all, a challenge to live a life of deep intimacy with Christ.

One of the most moving moments at an ordination is when the man becoming a priest or deacon prostrates himself, lying flat on the ground. It expresses his willingness to say "yes" to God's call and place his entire existence before the Lord. This prostration is a powerful symbol of the spirituality asked of a priest throughout his ministry. It is that of one who is called to be a shepherd, willing to lay down his life.

Earthenware Vessel

In his Second Letter to the Corinthians, St Paul talks of his ministry. He describes himself and others who are ministers of the Church as being 'earthenware vessels' that hold God's treasure (2 Corinthians 4:7). By this he means that compared to God and the gospel message, those called to be leaders in the Church are still only humble servants. The message is far more important than the messenger.

One thing that is common to all priests is that they know that they are not worthy of this great calling. Even St Peter says "Leave me Lord, I am a sinful man" (Luke 5:8) in a moment when he particularly recognises his own weakness in the presence of Christ. When a man is considering a vocation to priesthood, it is quite natural for him to ask the question "Why me, Lord?" This is because he recognises that, like any other man, he is far from perfect. Yes, God has given him wonderful gifts to be used throughout his life, but he is also a human being with all that this means in terms of sin, fragility, self-doubt and brokenness. The question however, is not really 'Am I worthy?' or 'Am I gifted enough?' but rather 'Is God calling me?', because this is what really matters. If God calls someone to a particular vocation, then he chooses them as there are, with all their strengths and weaknesses. He will give them the graces they need to fulfil that vocation. Of course this doesn't mean that they can just sit back and let God do all the work; they still have to use the gifts and time he gives them as best they can.

The challenge of an individual priest being a living icon of Jesus Christ as Head, High Priest and Shepherd is a daunting one. How can a man even begin to adequately imitate the Lord? The answer is because that is what God intended and what he calls individuals to do. Just as in marriage, the deep love of husband and wife is often shown in small things, so too with the Church. In the sacraments Christ becomes present through small things like a few drops of water or in bread and wine. The same is true of the priesthood – God uses ordinary people to do an extraordinary work for him.

The late Cardinal Hume, former Archbishop of Westminster, once said: "I have often thought that Our Lord chose a lot of Division Two people as priests. We can all think of better people among the laity than we know ourselves and we know our frailties and our weaknesses. I sometimes think he has deliberately chosen the earthenware vessels to be quite certain that the strays and

"I sometimes think he has deliberately chosen the earthenware vessels to be quite certain that the strays and failures will have someone who will understand and be sympathetic, and not condemn"
The late Cardinal Basil Hume *(right)*

failures will have someone who will understand and be sympathetic, and not condemn". (Light in the Lord, 1991, page 61). "If we look at the apostles, and even those called in the Old Testament to be prophets, many of them were not what we might call 'professional religious people' with theological training." We know that some of the apostles were fishermen, one a tax-collector and so on. Amos the prophet was a farmer and shepherd.

There are occasions, however, during Jesus' ministry when he has to remind the apostles not to get too proud or headstrong. We hear in St Luke's gospel that an argument broke out between the apostles as to who was the greatest (Luke 9:46). In response Jesus puts a little child before them and tells them that they should be like children. In St Mark's Gospel (Mark 10:35) the mother of James and John approaches Jesus asking that they have thrones at the Lord's side in heaven. Jesus' reply is that these are not his to grant, and that following him is about suffering, not personal glory. He then goes on to point out that they, like him, should behave like a servant not a master.

Archbishop Oscar Romero of El Salvador once said of those in ministerial service in the Church, "We are the workers, not the master builder; we are ministers, not messiahs; we are prophets of a future not our own."

In a sermon preached at ordinations celebrated in Rome during Eastertide in 2006, Pope Benedict XVI spoke about the humility needed to be a priest. During his homily, the Holy Father recalled the day's gospel reading, which was that of Christ the Good Shepherd, who gives his life for his flock. The priestly spirit, Pope Benedict stressed, is opposed to "careerism, the attempt to arrive 'high up', to seek out a position through the Church, to serve oneself and not serve others." He went on to say that to be a priest is not "to desire to be someone important, ... but to live for others, for Christ, and through him and with him to live for the men and women he seeks, whom he wants to lead along the path of life."

At his ordination ceremony, the man who is to become a priest prostrates himself on the floor as a sign of submission to God and of humility. This gesture becomes part of his spirituality as a priest and is a reminder to him of God's power working through him in his ministry rather than anything he achieves through his own efforts.

Bishop and Priest

Although a priest is uniquely and individually configured to Christ through his ordination, he is not his own man. The priesthood was instituted by Our Lord to serve the Church community and the world, and therefore the call to priesthood is not a call to personal fulfilment – a man is not a priest for himself, but for others.

The apostles were not only the first priests, but also the first bishops. In the early days of the Church the two offices were not separated. It was only in subsequent centuries that the sacrament of ordination developed into the three-fold ministry of deacon, priest and bishop. Today those ministries are clearly defined in the Church, though all exist within the one sacrament of order, not three separate sacraments.

The bishop is the chief pastor in the diocese. He exercises the ministry of teaching, sanctifying and ordering the diocese entrusted to his care, reflecting Christ's own roles as prophet, priest and king. The priest is described in the documents of Vatican II as a 'co-worker' with the bishop, and as such, the two collaborate in a spirit of openness and generosity.

The Canon Law of the Latin Rite Church (i.e., the Roman Church) legislates that a priest must be joined to, or to use the exact term, 'incardinated into', a particular diocese or religious community recognised by the Church. In other words, a priest must be under the jurisdiction of a bishop or superior; he cannot be an itinerant priest doing just as he likes.

There are good reasons for this, both theologically and pastorally. If the priest has been ordained for the good of the whole Church he needs to be formally united to it in some way. Also, lessons of history show that a priest needs to belong to a particular community for reasons of good order within the Church and also for the priest's own welfare. Although this might sound rather legalistic, there is also an important spiritual bond that exists between a diocesan priest and his bishop. A bishop is more than a priest's superior, he is a father in Christ, and the bond that exists between him and his priests carries two-way responsibilities.

At his ordination, the priest places his hand between those of the bishop and makes a promise of obedience to the bishop and his successors. This is done

"There is an important spiritual bond between a diocesan priest and his bishop... a bishop is more than a priest's superior, he is a father in Christ, and the bond that exists between him and his priests carries two-way responsibilities"

for reasons other than to help the bishop to administer the diocese smoothly – it is an act whereby the priest becomes bound to his bishop in a special way, and also joins his brother priests in a diocesan presbyterate.

Once a priest is incardinated into a diocese he has responsibilities towards that community to serve it well. His promise of obedience means that he must be willing to go wherever his bishop sends him and to undertake the tasks entrusted to him as a priest. It is also the case that the community and its leader, the bishop, has responsibilities to the priest. Just as the priest has pledged his life to serve God and the community, so the community has a responsibility to ensure that the life-needs of a priest are met, both while he is actively ministering and also when he is ill or when old age prevents him from undertaking a fully active ministry.

At his ordination, the priest receives an unrepeatable sacrament which changes him forever. As such this means that a validly ordained priest never stops being a priest. He never really retires as such, nor can he stop being a priest or be stripped of his priestly identity. In extreme cases, he can be dismissed from office, or stop exercising his priestly functions, but he is still a priest – forever.

Not my Will, But Yours be Done

Every follower of Jesus is asked to "renounce himself and take up his cross" (Matthew 16.24). For those who followed Jesus as apostles that meant quite a radical change of life. They left everything to follow him, including home and employment.

Jesus himself knew what it was to make sacrifices for the Kingdom of God. Philippians 2:6-11 tells us that Christ 'emptied' himself to come amongst us and that he was humbler still in accepting death on a cross. In the garden of Gethsemane, the night before he was crucified, Jesus prayed to His Father that "This cup might pass me by. Nevertheless, let it be as you not I would have it." (Matthew 26:39). In this prayer, the Lord offers his life completely to the Father. One who wishes to become a priest must also be willing to make sacrifices in imitation of his Master.

At his ordination as a deacon or as a priest, a man makes special promises: those of obedience and celibacy. He is also expected to live a relatively simple lifestyle. These are similar to, but not quite identical to, the vows that religious men and women take at their profession of poverty, chastity and obedience.

The promise of obedience is more than a commitment to simply follow the orders of the bishop. It is about putting one's whole life at the service of God and the Church in a positive attitude. Because Catholic priests do not marry and do not have children, they are free to go where the bishop sends them, according to pastoral need. Normally this would be inside the diocese to which he belongs, but occasionally priests are asked to work farther afield in special ministries. During the course of his ministry, a priest might be expected to move several times to different parish communities. No one would pretend that such moves are easy because a priest becomes attached to the people he serves and *vice versa*. Sometimes a priest might be moved because he has gifts that can be used profitably to help another parish. Sometimes he might be moved because the bishop feels that he needs him elsewhere because another priest has retired or had to move too.

Some people might see obedience as imposing a severe restriction on an individual's freedom, but that is not how the Church views it. The promise of obedience is there to free a man to work selflessly for the Kingdom. He is called to leave behind his own personal preferences and ambitions and to place himself in the hands of the Lord. He is not to see his priesthood as something that is his personal property, but rather as a gift to the Church that really belongs to Christ.

The promise of celibacy that a priest is required to make is linked to the promise of obedience and also to living a simple lifestyle, as all three are about the complete giving of self and being free for service. To be celibate simply means not to be married. However, its meaning is understood in broader terms, to include forsaking any type of relationship heading towards marriage, or akin to it. A priest is called to live chastely like all Christians, whatever their state of life. It is important to stress that celibacy is a requirement of the Latin Church, not something that is inextricably tied to the nature of priesthood itself. There are in fact a few married priests in England and Wales. These were men who were both married and in active ministry in non-Catholic communities before being received as Catholics. The Holy Father gave these men exceptional permission to be ordained as married Catholic priests.

The Church's requirement of celibacy has been much debated in recent years, not least because some men find that this requirement is too much of a personal sacrifice in order to become a priest. It is also the case that some priests have met someone they deeply love and have left active ministry in order to get married. The rule of priestly celibacy has not existed as a requirement for ordination since apostolic times. There is certainly evidence in the scriptures that many men who held the office of presbyter were, in fact, married, though it is also the case that both Jesus and St Paul prized celibacy for the sake of the Kingdom. The beginnings of the universal requirement for a celibate priesthood in the Latin Rite probably dates from 300AD onwards.

But why is the priest asked to sacrifice the intimate love of a wife, the joy of a family of his own, and God's great and beautiful gift of sexual intercourse? Is this just a Church law that has to be accepted reluctantly?

Part of the answer lies in how we understand the identity of a priest. He doesn't just share in Jesus' ministry; he shares in Jesus' life, as a man set apart. There can be little doubt that Jesus was celibate. This was a sign of his total dedication to his mission from the Father. He was single-minded and single-hearted in his commitment to his vocation. This doesn't mean that Jesus didn't love others, or let them love him; in fact the reverse is true. His celibate life was an expression of his complete love for the Father and the people he ministered to.

The challenge for the celibate priest is to love God and his people at the deepest level and to let that love shine through for others to see. As a priest, he is called to demonstrate the love of Jesus by word and deed, and to let others experience the love of God in their lives. In other words, far from being a denial of love, priestly celibacy opens the door to a different kind of love – the love of the Good Shepherd for his flock.

This does mean that a priest must have a healthy attitude not only to celibacy, but also to the love that exists within a marriage. Celibacy is not, in fact, the opposite of marriage; it is rather a different way of loving. A celibate priest should not turn himself into an unloving and unfeeling bachelor.

Anyone considering the priesthood must therefore weigh up in their minds whether they feel they have the gift of being able to embrace the celibate lifestyle. This does not simply mean that they have to make a decision to sacrifice marriage. They also need to consider the person that they are, their sexuality and maturity, how they will relate to other adults and how they will demonstrate love and affection in appropriate ways.

There will be pain in celibacy. Our society finds it strange and there will be times of pressure. There may also be occasions where a priest experiences a sense of loneliness and deprivation, especially when he sees friends and parishioners finding joy and happiness in marriage and family. At times like this, it is important to recognise that Jesus himself must have experienced similar feelings. Today, in our highly-sexualised world, there will be those who feel that celibacy is somehow unnatural. There are others, however, who believe that the celibate love of a priest has a special place as a visible sign witnessing to the love of God.

Whereas those who join religious congregations take a vow of poverty, those in diocesan priesthood do not; however, they are expected to live out gospel values, which includes living a way of life that is not centred on accumulating riches or material goods. The Code of Canon Law states "Clerics are to follow a simple way of life and avoid anything that smacks of worldliness." (Code of Canon Law 282/1). This simplicity of life is not quite the same as the vow religious take. Whereas members of a religious order usually hold things in common and have no personal property or savings, diocesan priests are not forbidden to have personal possessions. Of course, no one enters the priesthood to become rich – if they did they would be sadly disappointed! By the same token, priests are not expected to live in poverty and fail to take care of themselves. What would be important is that a priest is not excessively preoccupied with his income, accommodation or material well-being.

Most priests would never own a house or flat themselves, but would instead live in provided accommodation, normally in a house attached to the church where they serve. This house would often double-up as a parish office and also parish meeting room. Even in retirement, many priests live in a church-owned property rather than having their own home.

Priests' incomes vary. Some dioceses ensure that all their priests receive a modest monthly salary, whereas other dioceses operate a system whereby a priest's income is not fixed, but is reliant instead on the donations of parishioners. Normally the costs associated with a priest's living accommodation, such as heating and electricity, would be met by the parish, as would food. A priest is treated the same as any other resident in the United Kingdom, in that if his income is sufficient, he pays tax like everyone else.

The Prayer and Spirituality of a Priest

In St John's Gospel, chapters 15-17, Jesus gives a series of 'farewell' discourses to his apostles. We might sum up these by saying that to be a follower of Jesus means that we should be **in** the world, but not **of** the world. In other words we are not to live in a way which denies the reality of where we are, but that we should rather live where we are in an unworldly way, with our hearts and minds focused on God and his ways. This tension is at the heart of priestly spirituality, especially for a diocesan priest. On the one hand, the priest is to live in the midst of the community and serve it, and on the other he is a man of God. Of

course, these two states are not contradictory. When a priest is called from the community to serve God and his people, he is not called to be apart from the community but to live in it in a distinct way.

A diocesan priest will be at the rock face of life. He will share in many of the important moments of his parishioners'

> "A diocesan priest will be at the rock face of life. He will share in many of the important moments of his parishioners' lives and should be an important member of the local community"

lives and should be an important member of the local community, witnessing and serving not only to Catholics, but also to people of other faiths or none.

The diocesan priest, unlike members of some religious orders, is not called to live in an enclosed setting away from the world; rather he is to be at the heart of life, with all its problems and successes, and all its joys and sorrows. This requires a certain type of spirituality which is different from that of many of those who are religious life and follow the rule of their founder.

If a priest is to be a good shepherd and leader of the community of believers he must, like Jesus, have a life of prayer. The gospels tell us that Jesus often spent many hours in prayer, especially when he was at his busiest. It was as if he drew his strength in ministry from his prayer. When faced with the realities of a busy world, a priest can make only one of two choices; he can either embroil himself in the work to be done and ignore prayer, or he must find the time to pray in the midst of the work.

Not unreasonably, people will expect a priest to spend time in prayer. That is one of the things that they would see his spiritual fatherhood to include. He must not only lead publicly-said prayers, but also lead through personal prayer. He must be a man with a genuine spirituality. A priest who is so busy with the work of the Lord that forgets the Lord of the work is liable to burn out.

Many authors have written about the spirituality of a diocesan priest. One thing that is clear is that the history of the Church and its breadth of experiences in prayer have led to a multiplicity of spiritualities, with no single one being identifiable as the sole and authentic spirituality of the diocesan priest. Different people find that different types of prayer are more suited to them.

Nevertheless, there are certain hallmarks of prayer that we can point to as being present in the typical spirituality of a diocesan priest. There would be prayer and reflection around the promises that a priest makes at his ordination and an acceptance of these in daily life in a spirit of joyful sacrifice. Secondly, the centrality of the Eucharist and prayerful devotion towards Christ's presence in the sacrament. There would also be a joyful and genuine attempt to live out the values of the gospel and an acknowledgment of the failure to do this from time to time, and subsequent reception of the sacrament of reconciliation.

A priest is also required to pray the Divine Office, a series of structured and set prayers, which are said at various times throughout the day. There would also be traditional Catholic devotion to the saints and Blessed Virgin Mary, as well as more modern practices, too. Spiritual reading would also help a priest to focus his prayer life and give food for thought.

Not surprisingly, there would also undoubtedly be prayers of intercession and petition to God, based on the priest's contact with his parishioners and listening to their stories.

The varied ministries and the flexibility needed in the life of a diocesan priest means that finding time for prayer is very much in the priest's own hands. Some find that morning is the best time for prayer, others, the evening, when work is done. Whatever prayers a priest uses and whenever he prays, he would be mindful to remember the final promise he makes at his ordination and his response to this.

The bishops asks, "Are you resolved to consecrate your life to God for the salvation of his people, and to unite yourself more closely everyday to Christ the High Priest, who offered himself for us to the Father as a perfect sacrifice?" The candidate replies, "I am, with the help of God". Whatever a priest does, he doesn't do completely on his own energies and wishes. He is called to be *alter Christus* – another Christ. With this comes recognition that it is Christ working in him and through him that makes him what he is, and brings his work to fruition.

"Whatever a priest does, he doesn't do completely on his own energies and wishes... he is called to be *alter Christus* – another Christ"

Chapter

4

What does a Priest do?

The Challenge of Ministry today

The world in which we live has changed considerably in the last 50 years. Scientific and technological advances have improved the lives of many. Transport systems, particularly air travel, makes visiting the furthest parts of the globe a real option – something our great-grandparents could only dream about. People have such choice at the supermarket, in careers and in leisure opportunities.

Yet, this is not true the world over. Many people still live in poverty, which in many cases seems to be getting worse. New technologies bring new moral problems as well as benefits. Opportunities for the mass movement of people, often over great distances, raise issues of immigration and environmental concerns. Global terrorism is a new threat, as is the spread of diseases such as H.I.V., while new weapons have changed how wars are fought.

Things have also changed for the Church. Not only does it have to face the realities mentioned above like everyone else, but it also has factors of its own to deal with. In many parts of the world the Catholic population has considerably increased and the numbers of those applying for priesthood has also increased; however, in other parts of the world, including the United Kingdom, the number of those in church congregations and applying for the priesthood has gone down. These issues raise questions, such as how we should live as a Church community today and how we can best communicate the Gospel in our particular circumstances.

After the Second World War, the Catholic community saw an unprecedented rise in growth. The numbers in the seminaries were high and new church buildings were being erected in many places. This period of growth was atypical of what had gone before and was not destined to continue. Since the late 1960s there has been a steady decline in regular church attendance and the Catholic community is not as homogenous as it once was. This raises many issues, not least what it means to be a Catholic today and also what it means to be a priest in our society.

However, it is not all gloom and doom. There is increasing evidence that many in our society are questioning the worldly values that they have been brought up with as a result of increasing secularisation. They question whether personal self-worth is really something that can be measured by money and possessions, and whether the traditional models of family, so quickly discarded by many, might really have something to offer. Bookshops have many shelves full of books about spirituality, and many are hungering for meaning in their lives, even if they don't turn in the first instance to the Church.

The Catholic Church in this country has also been blessed in many regions with the arrival of immigrants, who bring their own characteristic style of Catholicism with them. There are also large numbers of laypeople who are willing to get involved in the life of their parishes. Women have taken on more roles in the Church. Young people who are practising their faith show signs of a real, deep and genuine commitment and a willingness to share this with others. After several decades of decline, fresh confidence is empowering many to more eagerly spread the faith in a more explicit way.

All of this means that the Church still has a vital role to play in our society, even if it is one different to what happened in the past. The priesthood, too, will continue to play an important part in Church life, even if some aspects of it will be expressed in slightly different ways than in years gone by.

The Church also has other issues to deal with, many of which are structural.

Picture courtesy of JOHN ROSS

Many churches, especially those in some town and city centres, are not operating at full capacity and yet still have big bills to pay for maintenance. Keeping the same number of churches and yet having fewer priests means that some priests now have to be shared between parishes. No one knows how things will develop in future years; it is in God's hands. However, anyone considering a vocation to the priesthood today needs to consider how they will adapt to change and put their faith in the Lord accordingly.

One of the greatest contributions that the Catholic community has made to the life of the country is its establishments of faith schools. These were initially independent of the state's provision of education, and served some of the poorest areas. In the 1940s, various denominations, including the Catholic community, agreed to collaborate with the government so that the country could provide free education for all. Church schools kept their individual identity, but also become part of wider state provision.

In this, and other ways, the Church continues to play a role in the wider community and shows that it is not self-serving. The Church is called to be a communal icon of God's love and care, a parable of community and the living gospel for all to hear.

Another facet of Church life today is that of ecumenism, that is the recognition and sharing of the common Christian faith that we have with other communities. Today, a priest is called to work in partnership with ministers of other Christian communities as appropriate. While divisions may exist, and these need to be honestly recognised, it is also the case that a lot of work can be done together, particularly social welfare activities to help those in need. In this way, we begin a journey together which hopefully will lead one day to a unity that will reflect more perfectly the reconciling love of God. It is also the case that dialogue and co-operation is needed with non-Christian people of faith in our multi-cultural and multi-faith society. Far from being on the decline, religion needs to recognised as a major force in our country today.

There are certainly many areas where Christians and other faith communities agree, particularly on issues of family life and the dignity of the human person. In all of this we need to remember that the priest is called to reflect Jesus, who had a concern for all people, not just those closest to him. There is much that can be gained and discovered if people choose to make their common life and faith journeys together.

A creative tension within the Church is how it can be both faithful to the unchanging eternal truths it teaches and also relevant to the people of our age. Even though it seems contradictory, we can say that it is always changing, yet always the same. It is the same in that its teaching and practice is faithful to that of Jesus and the apostles, and that it is changing in the way this teaching is explained and lived out over the centuries. If this is true of the Church as a whole, it is also true of the priesthood.

Serving Together – Collaboration with all

The fact that the number of priests in the England and Wales has fallen over recent decades has led the laity to a greater involvement in the life of the Church. While this has partly happened out of necessity, it has also happened because lay people have been encouraged to use their skills and talents to serve the Church. It would be wrong to think that lay people should only be there to help the priest, or do things he is too busy to do, as if they were 'plugging a gap'.

> "The priest is there to help people to discern, develop and use their creative gifts, so that they can flourish as a community of active Christians"

During the Second Vatican Council, the role of the laity was considered at length, and as a result, the unique and distinctive role of lay Christians was promoted. It should be noted, however, that this involvement was meant to include the role of the layperson in the mission of the Church in the wider world, not only taking responsibility for things that happen in the life of the parish.

We are encouraged to think about the unique part that everyone can play in the Body of Christ in our work of building up the Kingdom. The image we should have in our minds is that of a ministering community, not a community of ministers. In other words, it is about the whole Body of Christ collaborating together, rather than everyone just doing their own thing.

All current day statements from Rome on the ordained priesthood begin with an affirmation of the royal priesthood of all the baptised, and a call to an active sharing in the Church's worship and mission by every member, each in his or her own way. The reality is that the ordained priesthood serves the common priesthood. One benefit of the greater emphasis on the common priesthood of all the baptised is that it has brought into sharper focus the essential attributes of the ministerial (or ordained) priesthood. Another benefit is that priests often feel more supported and involved when they are collaborating with others.

The model that is emerging is one that recognises the ordained priest's ministry to nourish, lead and build-up the community which is comprised of individual members with their many different vocations, talents and ways of service. The priest is there to help people to discern, develop and use their creative gifts, so that they can flourish as a community of active Christians. So we can say that the ordained priest is not simply ministering to passive Christians, but rather is empowering them to more fully live out their baptismal vocation.

Picture courtesy of JOHN ROSS

In some parishes, lay people have been employed as parish workers. This role is more than being a secretary or mere helper. The role of parish worker (or parish pastoral assistant) would include some responsibility for the faith-life of the local community, perhaps by visiting homes or in leading programmes of sacramental preparation.

Serving together with lay people is not the only group of people a priest has to collaborate with. Many parishes have permanent deacons in them and also religious houses of sisters, priests and brothers. Permanent deacons at first appear to be a fairly new ministry in the Church. In fact, it is a very ancient ministry resurrected for our times. Permanent deacons can be either single or married men who are ordained as a deacon, without the specific intention of then becoming priests. Deacons can baptise, officiate at marriages and funerals, and preach at Mass; they cannot, however, preside at Mass or hear confessions. The permanent diaconate is now a major feature in many dioceses in the country, with deacons taking on diocesan roles in many cases. For the most part, deacons are attached to the parish where they and their families live. As a general rule, they do not tend to be asked by the bishop to move in the same way as priests do, though in theory they could be asked to do so.

Houses of men or women religious exist within the boundaries of many parishes. As such, even though they might enjoy an independent status, there is normally a good deal of contact between the local priest and those who live in the religious community. In some cases the parish might actually be run by priests from a religious order, rather than diocesan clergy. There are also a good number of parishes where sisters work as parish pastoral assistants, while still belonging to their own communities.

Even in the cases where religious are not directly involved with the parish, the call to communion in the Church demands that the priest have a fraternal care for them. Over the centuries, religious have played an indispensable role in the life of the Church. In our own country, many sisters and brothers ran schools and retreat centres over the years. Some are still involved in this work. Religious are also becoming increasingly involved in other kinds of pastoral work, including hospitals, universities and prison chaplaincies.

The Bishop and the Diocesan Presbyterate

A priest's relationship with his local bishop is very important. An earlier section has already explained why this is the case. In addition to his relationship with the bishop, a priest is also bound to his fellow co-workers, the priests of his diocese. Collectively, this group of priests is known as the "diocesan presbyterate".

Even if a priest lives on his own, serving his local community, he still remains part of a larger brotherhood which includes being a member of the diocesan presbyterate and of the local deanery. There are plenty of opportunities for getting together with fellow priests, perhaps meeting in small groups for prayer or simply for enjoying each other's company. Support and care for other priests is an important part of one's priestly ministry.

Most priests begin their years of service as an assistant priest in a parish. Here they serve with a more experienced priest and other members of a parish. This gives them the opportunity to learn and share what it means to be a priest. More and more emphasis is placed on the on-going, indeed lifelong, formation that takes places after ordination. In some places, different ways of working together with other priests is being tried. Sometimes a team of priests might live in the same house and serve several churches. In other places priests have simply chosen to gather together once a week for prayer and a meal to support each other in their life and work. One of the essential attributes of a priest therefore is having the ability and desire to relate well with others and to work not only for them, but with them. The priest must cherish others and weave together their vocations and gifts in to a seamless robe for the service of the Lord.

Priest

Through baptism we all share in the priestly, kingly and prophetic offices of Christ. For an ordained, ministerial, priest, these offices take on a new significance. It is not that this three-fold sharing in Christ's life changes in a symbolic way, rather that through ordination there is a real difference, a change in "essence and degree" as the Second Vatican Council reminded us.

The single most identifiable duty of a priest is that of presiding at the Eucharist. Only a priest has the power to effect the change whereby bread and wine become the Body and Blood of Christ, through the power of the Holy Spirit in the celebration of the Mass. It is as celebrant of Mass that most people will regularly encounter a priest.

Traditionally, especially in the Old Testament, a priest is one who offers sacrifice. Christ exercised his priesthood on the Cross as he offered his life to the Father as a perfect sacrifice. Today, in the Mass, that sacrifice is re-presented to the Father through the power of the priest.

It would not be unfair to describe the priest as being "a man of the Eucharist". For the Church, as well as being a sacrifice, the Eucharist has other significances, too. Sharing a meal with his apostles was central to Jesus' life. The Passover meal on the night before he died was the last of many suppers with his friends. It was a meal of fellowship. In the same way the Church views the Mass as a sign of fellowship and belonging; indeed, more than that – it is a sign of the communion we have with each other as the Body of Christ. And so in celebrating the Mass, the priest not only offers Christ's sacrifice; he is also calling the community into communion with God and one another.

There is no greater or humbling ministry for a priest. In the Eucharist he is the

Picture courtesy of JOHN ROSS

living icon or image of Jesus as our great high priest. Just as the Church describes the Eucharist as the source and summit of Christian life (Second Vatican Council: *Lumen Gentium 11*), so in a special way it is the source and summit of a priest's life, too. Everything else flows from the Eucharist and leads back to it, and it is in the Eucharist, above all else, that we see the priest's role most clearly expressed.

> "The Church has traditionally listed seven events of sacramental action – Baptism, Confirmation Eucharist, Marriage, Priesthood, Reconciliation and Anointing of the Sick"

The Eucharist is not, however, the only sacrament a priest celebrates. At the very heart of the Catholic faith is the truth that God touches our lives through signs and gestures, in a way suited to us as human beings. We use signs and symbols all the time to express our inner selves to others, making the invisible present through something visible, for example, our deep hidden love for another can be demonstrated through the giving of a gift. This is a naturally human way of reaching out to others, flowing from the way God made us. God has chosen this way, too, so that he can touch our lives. This is at the heart of what a sacrament is.

The sacraments are the deepest and richest signs of all. In them the risen Christ is personally present to us through the ministry of the Church. They do not limit him in what he does, but they are central, visible ways in which he acts. The sacraments are the personal touch of Jesus, often at key moments of our lives. They are powerful instruments of the Good News, Jesus himself.

The Church has traditionally listed seven events of sacramental action, (Baptism, Confirmation Eucharist, Marriage, Priesthood, Reconciliation and Anointing of the Sick). In addition, the Church itself, of its very nature, is also sacramental. Jesus himself is present in the sacraments, just as the invisible God became present as a human being in the wonder of the incarnation.

In a parish, the sacraments will provide key moments in the weekly ministry of a priest. He will celebrate daily Mass in the church, as well as perhaps in a school or even people's houses. Every Sunday is centred on several celebrations of the Eucharist. Often on a Sunday there are infants to be baptised. During the week he may anoint the sick at home or in hospital. Usually on a Saturday, time is set aside for reconciliation, but he is always ready to celebrate this sacrament at other times, too. Also on Saturdays weddings are often celebrated, bringing together a loving couple in a way that mirrors Christ's love for his Church. Many of these sacraments require preparatory work, and often it will be the priest himself who prepares others to receive the sacraments.

We can see why celebrating the sacraments are so central to a priest's ministry. The priest proclaims the presence of Christ in the sacraments. He is an agent of personal contact for the people with Jesus himself. And it is above all in the sacraments that the priest himself is a living sacrament of the Good Shepherd. It is Jesus himself who really ministers the sacraments. When the priest baptises, consecrates, anoints or absolves, it is the Lord himself who is at work, and so he continues his work of salvation through his priests.

All the sacraments are in some way linked to Jesus' ministry and all have been instituted by him. At the end of St Matthew's gospel (Matthew 28.19), Jesus commands his apostles to baptise all nations. He forgave sinners who repented (Luke 5:20, John 8:11). Today he sends his priests to anoint the sick, as once he sent his apostles (Mark 6:13. See also James 5:14-15).

Prophet

Even though the sacraments are so important in the life of priests, no priest would want to be seen solely as someone who just administers the sacraments. There is much more to priesthood than this. As well as healing and touching people's lives, Jesus also proclaimed the Good News and spoke of God to the world. This is very much the role of a prophet. A prophet is not so much a person who predicts the future; rather, they are someone who tells others of God's desires and commands. They are not so much 'fore-tellers' as 'forth-tellers'!

In the celebration of the Mass, there are two distinct, but united liturgies: the Liturgy of the Word and the Liturgy of the Eucharist. The former includes the readings in the first part of the Mass. After the readings have been proclaimed at Sunday Mass, the priest, or sometimes the deacon, gives a considered reflection about the readings and how these relate to our lives today. This is often called the homily or sermon. When the priest does this he is exercising his prophetic ministry, i.e., proclaiming God's Word.

However, this prophetic ministry is not confined to the pulpit on Sunday. There may be many times during a week when a priest is called to bear witness to God and his ways; perhaps in a school assembly, or local meeting. These days this might include a radio interview or providing a 'Thought for the Day' in a local newspaper. Some priests even provide a weekly reflection on the internet. In all of these, the priest is saying something to others about God and the fullness of life he offers if we live by his commandments. It is not that the priest is simply talking about his own opinions or feelings; rather, he is faithfully presenting gospel values and the teaching of the Church, which is the living voice of Jesus in the world today.

The People of God are not called to mediocrity. Rather, they are called to be what God gives them the potential to be. This includes having as full a knowledge and understanding of God and his love for them as each individual can. This does not equate to a dry, sterile intellectual understanding, but rather a dynamic living faith that touches daily life. Part of a priest's prophetic role includes explaining the faith and encouraging the people entrusted to him to reflect on God's presence and its meaning. This will also include teaching people about practical aspects of Church life and belief especially the Church's moral teaching.

Above all, a priest must try to make his whole life one of prophetic witness rather than just using words. Setting a good example is as crucial in helping people in knowledge of God as is a long theological treatise.

King

For many peoples of the ancient world, kingship was a common concept. At his trial in front of Pontius Pilate, Jesus is asked if he is a king. He replies that he is, though his kingdom is not of this world (John 18:36). When he is crucified, the charge sheet above him reads "Jesus of Nazareth, King of the Jews". For Jesus, his kingship was not exercised with the trappings of worldly pomp. His crown is of thorns; he rides on a donkey; he was born in a stable, not a palace. The model of kingship that Jesus gives is one of a genuine authoritative leadership, but lived out in a spirit of service; he is the Servant King and the Good Shepherd. Today the ministerial priest heads the local community in the name of Christ. Even if our understanding of worldly kingship has changed, the leadership that a priest gives must always be based on the example of Christ the King.

It is certainly clear that Jesus vested his apostles with a mission and authority akin to his own, which he did not give to other followers. It is also the case that not everyone can be leader; and yet leadership is needed, in many forms. In the past, many kings, being absolute monarchs, could exercise power without any accountability. This has never been the case in the Church. With authority comes accountability, not only within the visible structures of the Church, but to God himself.

If the priest is going to be an effective and proper leader of his local community, he must always remember that while he does so by the nature of the office to which he has been called, he must still give good example and have a real and genuine love of God and his people. To be a 'king' within the local community does not mean giving orders and commands, but following the gentle example of Jesus, who washed his apostles' feet.

Parish Ministry

The parish is where most people experience what it means to belong to the Church. Although there are various ministries for priests outside of parish life,

"If the priest is going to be an effective and proper leader of his local community... he must still give good example and have a real and genuine love of God and his people"

most priests spend their lives in parishes, occasionally moving as the bishop requests.

A parish is, above all else, a family. Other, more formal definitions exist which would include the fact that all parishes have clearly defined geographical boundaries. A parish is also an entity that encompasses the many different circumstances of those who belong to it, be they single or married, young or old, or any other permutation that ones cares to imagine. No two parishes are the same any more than any two families are the same. Each has its own unique circumstances, its own challenges and blessings.

An inner-city parish is very different to a rural one. Even in a single town or city there can be great diversity: one parish may have a strong multi-cultural dimension; one could be in relatively well-off suburbs while another may have serious problems of poverty and deprivation; one could have a sizeable student population and another several large hospitals. All parishes call for the same fundamental ministry of a priest, but each in its own distinctive way. The priest therefore needs to be flexible and adapt himself to the needs of each situation.

In any parish, the priest's ministry is to build-up a community of faith, or truly faith-filled people. It is in their parish that they encounter Jesus in the Scriptures, in the sacraments and in their fellow parishioners. A parish is not just meant to be a cosy community which comes together for an hour each week; it is rather to be a dynamic living expression of Church and of the Gospel in the locality. Neither does a parish exist just for itself; it is supposed to be a servant community for others, including those who do not formally belong to the Church. In short, it is to be a microcosm of everything that the universal Church is called to be.

One of the main tasks of priests working in parishes is to help people to discover the part God has given them to play in his work, and the gifts he has bestowed upon them. True pastoral leadership involves allowing people to become responsible members of the Church, creating a sense of participation and interdependence. While this is to be primarily exercised in the varied situation of people's daily lives, there are also times when it needs to be lived out within the Church community as well. Many parishes have active groups or teams involved in various facets of Church life. Some of these groups are traditional sodalities or clubs, but also newer ministries are being developed in many parishes. These may include things like bereavement support groups and marriage preparation teams. In some parishes people have chosen to join 'ecclesial movements' which have their own spirituality and activities.

The Rich Variety of Parish Life

Most priests adopt some kind of routine once they get used to parish life, but their ministry remains varied and somewhat unpredictable. The God who surprises never allows anyone to become too settled. The priest never really knows what the next call on his time will be, who will come to the door or who will make contact by phone or email. A priest can never really sit down at the end of a day in the knowledge that everything has been done. There are only so many hours in the day and a priest has his limitations as everyone else does. Jesus himself did not feed or cure everyone who came to him. A priest needs to prioritise and make judgments about what needs doing and when. When Jesus chose to visit Zacchaeus' house (Luke 19), he decided that this man needed him there and then. The gospels also give us the parable of the lost sheep, in which the shepherd leaves the 99 to search for one that had become separated. Perhaps today the priest might see it rather as leaving the one to search for the 99 who are lost! He cannot do this alone. He needs the support and help of his parish, and, above all, of God. The little a priest feels he has to offer can feed a multitude if blessed by the Lord.

A priest's entire ministry involves personal contact. Some of this will occur at the back of church after Sunday Mass, but also a priest will need to meet people on other occasions, maybe by visiting them at home. In years gone by, this was a mainstay of a priest's weekly activities; these days it has become more difficult as increasing demands take up a priest's time and also parishioners tend to lead far more active lives. Nevertheless, a priest needs to visit his parishioners if he is to be a good shepherd. He needs to have a special care for the sick, elderly and housebound. In all of this he should remember the example of Jesus who visited and encountered many people during his ministry. Jesus also said "Whoever welcomes you welcomes me" (Matthew 10:40) – to welcome a priest into one's home is to invite Jesus into it also.

Other Ministries

Ministry in a Hospital

Many priests serve hospitals in their parishes as part of their ministry, together with lay people, but some hospitals are so large that a full-time chaplain is needed.

Jesus showed compassion for the sick, and touched their lives in many ways, often simply by being with them. In a hospital, just as in a parish, the priest is there to bring the risen Christ to those to whom he ministers. As well as celebrating the sacraments and praying with the sick, his ministry will also touch the lives of the families of those who are ill and also the staff.

The chaplain is an important part of the care team in a hospital. The Church views a human person as an integrated whole, comprising the physical body, the mind and the spirit (soul). All three must be cared for and it would be wrong for healthcare professionals to neglect the spiritual needs of their patients.

There are also many ethical considerations in medicine today. Sometimes a priest might be invited to comment on moral issues, or even to lecture trainee

nurses on why the Church takes a particular stance on a medical or human life-issue.

Sometimes a priest will be called out during the night, particularly if a patient is close to death. Just as the hospital is operational 24 hours a day, seven days a week, so too the priest will make himself as available as possible, often with the help of other priestly colleagues.

It might also be the case that a priest is asked to care for those who are not so much ill, but rather disabled or who have other special needs. Some priests are able to celebrate Mass and preach using sign language for the deaf.

Ministry in a School or Sixth-Form College

Nearly every priest will be a part-time school chaplain at some time during his ministry. Often this will be in a Catholic primary school which serves the local parish. Sometimes it will be in a Catholic secondary school, which might include a sixth form, or in a college of further education. While all of these educational establishments are very different, when the priest goes into any of them he does so not as a teacher, but as a priest, ministering to pupils and their families, and also to staff.

In a school, a priest is very much part of a team which is interested in the welfare and development of the young people who attend. Unlike most hospitals and prisons, Catholic schools have their own distinctive ethos – they exist not only to help young people academically, but also to develop their faith.

In any Catholic school, the priest's role is similar to that in the parish: he will administer the sacraments, proclaim the Gospel and help to build a community of faith. Many schools also employ lay people in a chaplaincy capacity; it may well be that the priest only has a few hours a week in the school, while the lay chaplaincy assistant may be full-time.

Jesus was keen that children, as well as adults, had the opportunity to meet him. He reprimanded the apostles on one occasion when they tried to chase the little ones away (Matthew 19:13-15). Sometimes just being with Jesus was important. In the same way, a school chaplain can be quite effective, not by doing lots of things, but rather simply by being there and having time for others. This is particularly important for young people, especially teenagers, who are at an important time in their lives. They often value having someone there to accompany them; someone who understands their needs and concerns. The priest can play an important role in this regard, especially as he represents Jesus and the Church in a special way.

Higher Education Chaplaincy

Every university has a Catholic Chaplain; however, different chaplaincy models apply in each place due to the unique circumstances of each university. At its heart, the priest's ministry at a university is the same as anywhere else, but there are special challenges involved, too. Unlike Church-run schools, which are Catholic in nature, most universities are secular institutions; that is to say they do not see themselves existing for any specifically religious purpose. Nevertheless, most universities recognise that proper care of their students involves catering for their spiritual needs, and so local bishops are asked to appoint chaplains, either part-time or full-time. Like in many schools and parishes, lay people may also be on the chaplaincy team.

The time when young people leave home can be especially challenging. Some find the break quite difficult, whereas others revel in their new life with all its freedoms and variety – both can present difficulties. For many young Catholics, this will be the first time that they have lived outside of Catholic environments, such as the home and school. These people need special care and attention and a university chaplain is there to help.

At university, some people actually discover faith for the first time, or wish to explore their existing faith more deeply, so a chaplain must be willing to assist in this regard. Many foreign students will find the move to the United Kingdom a big culture shock; the Church can help them to adjust as well being an anchor point for them.

Most students are at university during term-time only, and for just three years. This means that the community at the university is always changing, with up to a third of the population leaving each year and being replaced by equally young people. This means that the university chaplain has to get accustomed to working in an environment quite different to a normal parish where there is more stability in the congregation and where the priest can call on people to collaborate with him with a long-term view.

It is also the case that young people's university experience sets them up for life in many different ways, including how they practise their faith. The university chaplain can do so much good in this regard and provide a valuable service at an important time in many people's lives. He can also help them with their own personal vocational discernment.

Ministry in a Prison

Just as every university in the country has a designated Catholic chaplain, so too do all the prisons and young offenders' institutions. Some are large enough to warrant a full-time priest chaplain and lay pastoral workers, others might just have a priest working part-time. In the parable of the sheep and goats (Matthew 25:36), "I was in prison and you visited me" is one of the hallmarks of the virtuous. Working with those in prison has always been an important part of the Church's pastoral work.

When a man or woman is sent to prison, it is often the case that they are "out of sight, out of mind". In other words, because they are locked away behind walls, the public (and often their families) do not always acknowledge their needs and difficulties. It is not easy for someone to admit to their problems when they are in prison because it might appear as weakness in front of fellow inmates. As a result they often bottle-up their emotions and thoughts and so create additional problems. While a prison chaplain is not there in a social work capacity, he can, and does, listen to the needs inmates have and can often do something to help.

It should also be remembered that inmates' families and children also suffer when they go to prison. Often a priest who works in a prison will find himself in contact with inmates' families. Also, as in schools and universities, the priest ministers to the staff, too.

The main tasks that a priest undertakes in prison are celebrating a weekly Mass and visiting prisoners, be they in their cells, in solitary, in the hospital wing or when they first arrive. Two important principles of Christianity are that people can change and that God will not desert them no matter what they have done. Part of a priest's work in prison, therefore, is to give people hope and encourage them to change and lead lives based on gospel values.

Ministering to the Armed Services

Jesus was ready and willing to go to the house of the Roman centurion to cure his servant (Matthew 8:6). Today, priests minister to members of the armed services and their families in his name. This can be as a full-time or part-time officiating chaplain. It should be noted that in the case of full-time chaplains, a priest will still ultimately belong to his own diocese and will only be considered for service several years after ordination.

Being a chaplain in the Army, Royal Navy or RAF is a special challenge. Although a non-combatant, a full-time priest chaplain is under military command and serves alongside those who are in these services – this can sometimes mean being in the theatre of war or living in places of political instability.

The chaplain ministers to a fairly mobile community, many of whom are in their late teens or twenties. Life in the armed services is understandably demanding, and often not just in the physical sense. A priest serving as a chaplain may find himself celebrating Mass anywhere from a permanent base to a ship or muddy field.

Padres, as they are often called by service personnel, have a long and distinguished tradition of standing alongside those to whom they minister in the most dangerous of circumstances; indeed, many have been killed in action or given awards for bravery. Being a military chaplain will, of its nature, involve dealing with death and injury, but also with the courage and comradary of those who are willing to lay down their lives for the good of others.

Diocesan Roles

In every diocese some priests are asked to undertake special ministries which serve the diocese as a whole. The bishop has his vicars general, chancellor and sometimes a private secretary. There is a priest responsible for promoting and directing priestly vocations and often a priest helps in the co-ordination of work with young people, perhaps even running a Catholic youth centre. Some priests may be asked to be part of the staff of a seminary or to serve the Church in another part of the world where there is a shortage of priests. Some priests also serve as port chaplains, especially to crew members who are away from home.

Presbytery Life

The house a priest lives is often called a presbytery. Although it doesn't actually belong to him, it is his home, and like any home, should be a place of welcome and security. When a priest is first ordained, he will generally share a presbytery with another priest, or sometimes several priests. Presbytery life is what those living there make of it, as is the case with any people sharing a home together. Sometimes a priest can get some domestic help, though live-in housekeepers are becoming very rare. More and more priests are choosing to cook for themselves, though many do get some help with cleaning and laundry.

Due to the nature of priestly ministry and often because of the size and location of the presbytery, it will never completely be his private space. The priest's house is, in many ways, the parish's house, too. It will often be used for meetings and welcoming people who want to see the priest. The parish office will usually be based there as well. All of the sacrifices that the priest is asked to make are intended to make him more open and available to those he serves, and this includes his house and home. Even if the presbytery is not literally

Faith across the seas: Priests serve the Church in a wide manner of roles,
including port chaplains to the many seafarers who visit the UK each year

Picture courtesy of the Apostleship of the Sea

'open house', it should always be a place of welcome.

The Work of the Lord

Despite what some people may think, it is not easy to be a priest. It has its own particular challenges, and these will be unique for each individual priest, based on the circumstances in which he finds himself ministering. Jesus told his followers that they must take up their cross and follow him daily.

In spite of all the difficulties, or perhaps because of them, the priesthood is a very rewarding way of life. Ministering to other people in the name of Jesus is a great privilege, and knowing that you have made a difference in people's lives is very rewarding.

The fact that there are so many different ways to serve as a priest means that there will be the opportunity to experience many different facets of life and work alongside people in very different circumstances. Even on a daily basis there will be some routine activities, but also many unknowns that need responding to. All of this requires a man with a generous heart, with a care and love for others, and with flexibility. Above all a priest must have a love of God and his ways.

Thomas Ken, an Anglican bishop living in the 17th century, wrote the following prayer, which has so much to say about the qualities needed in those who would be priests:

> *Give me the priest these graces shall posses:*
> *of an ambassador the just address,*
> *a father's tenderness, a shepherd's care,*
> *a leader's courage which the cross can bear,*
> *a ruler's arm, a watchman's wakeful eye,*
> *a pilot's skill, the helm in storms to ply,*
> *a fisher's patience and a labourer's toil,*
> *a guide's dexterity to disembroil,*
> *a prophet's inspiration from above,*
> *a teacher's knowledge and a Saviour's love.*

Chapter 5

What is it Really Like?

What is being a priest really like? That is a very fair question, and one to which anyone considering priesthood would want an answer. The reality is that every priest's life is slightly different and so it is difficult to give just one answer. However, to give an insight into one priest's personal vocation would perhaps give some indication of what it is like generally. A priest who has been ordained for a few years writes:

> FIRST HEARD my calling to be a priest when I was around 11 years old and to be honest I didn't have a clue how to respond. I continued my education at my local Catholic primary school in Derbyshire, before going on to St Benedict Catholic High School in Derby. I then studied politics at Loughborough University and, as is always the case with God's callings, he simply never lets go and the call to be a priest remained with me and continued to germinate.

However, now was not the time to respond, or so I thought and so, by way of an impulse decision, while in the university's careers library, I decided to begin a post-graduate course in law, with the intention of training to be a barrister. I was accepted to train at the Inns of Court in

London when, in the summer of my departure, I was quite shocked to discover a new-found confidence to actually respond to my real calling.

I don't have any doubts that it was the Holy Spirit who gave me the courage to pick up the phone and call a young priest in my diocese, whom I remembered meeting a few years previously, and have a chat about what to do with this calling.

I have now been ordained for three-and-a-half years and my decision to accept the call to be a priest has been one that I have never regretted. I am writing this during the season of Advent, a time when we're called to look out for the signs of the Kingdom being established in our lifetime. If I were to point to the most distinctive aspect of the priestly vocation it is the fact that we come into contact with these signs on a daily basis.

No day is what you might describe as typical, but celebrating Mass is the focal point of most days. Often, when I begin to take my vocation for granted, a word or phrase in the Mass texts suddenly hits me at an incredible level and provides a challenge to the whole day in trying to respond to it. I think it's actually the Holy Spirit nudging me to recognise that despite being the one wearing the colourful vestments and doing most of the talking, God remains in total control now and forever. Just before the priest begins to proclaim the Gospel and preach he says quietly "The Lord be in my heart and on my lips that I may worthily proclaim his Holy Gospel"; but it's one thing to say that it is God who is doing the talking and another thing entirely to believe it.

Fortunately for us, the Word became flesh, and so it's our ministry among people where I have truly recognised God's influence in the world as oppose to my own thoughts of influence. Many of my friends ask me whether the Sacrament of Reconciliation (or Confession) gets me down, but for me it's actually where I discover how good people really are despite occasions when the media portrays this otherwise. Listening to a confession is the place where I've discovered my own helplessness. I can't solve the vast majority of problems that people face, but then again the penitent doesn't expect me to. They are receiving the sacrament because they know God is the one who reconciles and the priest is the physical channel to that forgiveness and, hopefully, also a reminder to them of God's love.

It's also a tremendous privilege to accompany people through their grief following the death of a loved one. A 'privilege' because I've discovered just how strong many people's faith is. Death is not the end but is part of their future and despite the fact that many people have often not been to Mass for years, when they seek the priest's guidance through a funeral liturgy, the welcome that we can offer is God's welcome. In so doing we can participate in the living story of the Prodigal Son, where the Father always keeps his eye out for his loved ones.

Working with young people is yet another opportunity to recognise the signs of God's Kingdom being established in our world. To be fair, although young people often get a bad press, and although I may not see them all on a Sunday, their way of expressing faith is often unconventional. The overwhelming desire to establish justice in the world and offering support for those who face an extra challenge in life, whether this is poverty, disability or political oppression, is the characteristic I would most associate with many young people I have worked with. In many respects a school community is not merely a luxury extra to the life of a parish, but is central to its mission. Young people are not the future, they're the present and if you're open to the life-giving presence of the Holy Spirit, working with younger people is incredibly rewarding.

I mentioned previously that my response to God calling me to the priesthood really began to take shape when I received the Holy Spirit's gift of 'courage'. I have discovered that all the Spirit's gifts are essential to not just 'doing' the tasks of a priest but actually 'being' a priest. I hope I never take for granted the fact that a vocation is something that has to be worked at. In the same way that two teachers teaching the same year group can do so in totally different ways – one turning up at the required time, teaching a lesson impassively and leaving when the job is done is totally different from the teacher who teaches because they value their pupils' lives and gifts which they are called to nurture in the world – the priest faces the same challenge.

A vocation is a life that unfolds as we continue to be inspired by the people to whom we minister. We recognise the gifts of the Holy Spirit in others and gratefully accept that we need them to live out our vocation in our unique way. You might ask the question as to whether you really feel yourself suitable to being called, but let God be the judge of that. The discovery I made after finally having the courage to answer my call is that although it is not without its challenges, it is a great life. The priest has the opportunity to join others in living out their vocations and not only see the signs of God's Kingdom, but actually become a sign of it. What a life!

Chapter

6

Could it be me?

Am I Called?

Are you being called by Jesus? The answer is a clear "Yes!" Each of us is being asked to do something a little special for God. He has a task for you. He created you for a reason, with a lot of care, giving you special gifts and blessings. Jesus is calling you. You are already living your first vocation – to follow him, to be his disciple. But what special task is Jesus asking of you?

The Voice of the Lord

Jesus called his apostles in a very personal way. He went to them where they were, spent time with them and called them by name. He calls people to be priests in the same way today, but his presence and his voice are silent and mysterious. You are unlikely to hear a booming voice from on high saying, "Be my priest!" Your experience will probably be much the same as Elijah: he found God not in the mighty wind, the earthquake or the fire, but in the gentle breeze (1 Kings 19: 9-14).

Jesus comes to you and calls you in a way that never forces itself upon you. His voice reaches deep within you but leaves you totally free. You will hear that voice in the silence of your prayer, in the words of the Scriptures and in the words and lives of those around you. So often it is through a simple suggestion by another priest or someone else that the Lord first brings alive his call in a person's heart.

'Come and See' (John 1:39)

Jesus is with you where you are, at home, at work, college or school. It is there, in your ordinary daily life, that he will come to you. It is there that you must listen for his voice, and open yourself to whatever his call may be. If you ask Jesus, "What do you want of me?" he will say "Come and see". It is vital that you spend time with him in prayer and reflection. Then you are more likely to hear his voice in whatever way he calls to you.

No two people are the same, and Jesus approaches different people in different ways. He treats us as individuals. He will come to you in your particular circumstances, to you as God has made you and as you are now, with all your strengths and weaknesses. It is always Jesus who makes the first move: "You did not choose me; no, I chose you" (John 15:16). He already, now, puts his trust in you, and wants to entrust you with a special task – perhaps service as a priest.

A Strong Feeling

The first sign that Jesus may well be calling you to be a priest is a strong feeling deep within you. It is there that the voice of Jesus will reach, stirring you to listen more deeply and to discover his loving will for you in his Church.

You may already have had such feelings in the past. Perhaps you knew a priest who inspired you. Your attraction to the priesthood may have been very strong at one time, but it came and went. Now it is beginning to return, or perhaps you are having such feelings for the first time.

That feeling within you is very important! You may have had some great moment when you felt deeply called: perhaps on retreat, at Lourdes, at an ordination, watching a film or reading a book about the life of a priest, or as you saw the priest at Mass. What matters more is that your feeling grows into a settled sense that this is the Lord's will for you. It will need the test of time. You may have to wrestle with the idea over several years. Time will give you the

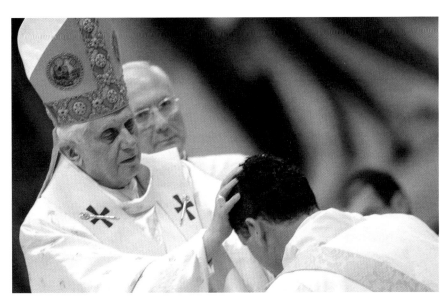

"There is no right to the priesthood. One cannot choose it as one chooses this job or that. One can only be chosen for it – by him"

Cardinal Ratzinger (now Pope Benedict XVI)

chance to look at your motives and to explore other options with an open heart. If in the end the persistent and surviving thought is the priesthood, that will be a strong indication that Jesus may well be calling you to be a priest.

"Let Your Will Be Done, Not Mine" (Luke 22:42)

Certainly Jesus is speaking to you, calling you. We are often not very good at recognising his call straight away. Like Samuel, we can mistake it for something else (1 Samuel 3:1-10). Sometimes after a deep conversion experience or a new enthusiasm at being received into the Church, we can mistake our strong sense of a call to dedicate ourselves to God, for a call to the priesthood. It may well be a call to serve as a dedicated lay person in some special way. You will need to listen very openly and humbly.

Any true disciple seeks not what 'I want' but what God wants. It is a sign of our love for the Lord who loves us. He may well place in your heart a deep desire to be a priest, and wanting to be ordained can be an important sign that the Lord is calling you. But a strong feeling or desire is not necessarily such a sign. We can mistake God's call, even when we are really committed to him. The apostles themselves were good examples of this.

The priesthood is not something I can pick out for myself or give myself. I cannot push myself forward for ordination, or seek it on my own terms. The Lord's call cannot be forced by my own desire or choice. It is pure gift. It is always a response to his summons, his call, his choice of me. No matter how strongly I would like to be a priest, it is his will that matters, not mine.

Before he became Pope in 2005, Cardinal Ratzinger published a collection of reflections on priestly spirituality entitled *Ministers of Your Joy* (1988). He said the following about those who would become priests:
> "There is no right to the priesthood. One cannot choose it as one chooses this job or that. One can only be chosen for it – by him. To be a priest does not belong to the list of human rights, and no one can sue to obtain it. He calls those whom he desires... For those who have received this call this means: He wants me. There is a will of Jesus concerned with me. I must enter into this will and mature within it. It is the space within which I must live. Our life will become the more fulfilled and free the more we become one with his will in which the most profound truth of our own self is contained."

A Surprising Choice

What God asks of us is often a surprise. You may think that you lack the gifts needed for priestly service, or that you already have those that are necessary. We are not always the best judges of the ways God has gifted us, and discovering our key gifts often takes time: they may not be what we think they are. You can imagine Peter's reaction to Jesus' call to him to be a 'rock' for others: "What me, a rock?"

You may find the growing feeling of a call to the priesthood very disturbing. You feel unworthy, unsuited, unable to cope. That is perfectly natural. You may have said "No" in the past, or be trying to say "Not now". Others have done the same. Peter's response was "Leave me, Lord, I am a sinful man" (Luke 5:8). Moses asked, "Who am I to do this?" (Exodus 3:11) and suggested that God ask someone else (Exodus 4:13). The Lord can cope with our "No", but he never takes back or regrets his choice (Romans 11. 29). What God asks of us is always too much, left to ourselves. Like Mary, mother of the Lord, it is natural for us to ask, "But how can this come about?" (Luke 1:34). God's response to us is the same as to Moses: "I will be with you" (Exodus 3: 12). And in our feeling of being unworthy and barren, he says to us as he said to Mary about Elizabeth and her future son, "Nothing is impossible to God" (Luke 1:37).

Into the Wilderness

As the Lord's call reaches deeper within us and begins to call forth a "Yes" in our hearts, we can expect to be tempted. As soon as Jesus was confirmed in his ministry at his baptism in the Jordan, he was led into the wilderness to be tempted away from his vocation (Luke 4: 1-13). The same will happen to you. Such temptations can either lead you to reject or distort God's call, or it can strengthen your resolve to discover and accept it as your vocation.

Called Through the Church

The path to ordination begins with the feeling that you would like to be a priest, that you are being called by the Lord. You explore the idea, pray about it and test it with time. But you still ask, "How can I be sure it is what God wants?" On your own, you cannot, no matter how strong the feeling inside you. God's call comes to your heart in a very personal way, but it comes to you as a member of the Church, through the Church and for the service of the Church.

Personal but not Private

Some people see the bond between us and God in very individualistic terms, as something rather private. They think of God calling people directly, without the Church. A vocation is something very personal, but it is never private. We need to go back to St Paul's great vision of the Church as the Body of Christ. We are all vital members, needing and needed by each other.

Jesus comes to us through the life of his Body, his community of faith. His gifts are for building up the Body of Christ. That community itself is the 'fullness of Christ', it is the way Jesus reaches the world and the way we ourselves meet him as his disciples. This is a very important point. We should not expect Jesus to call someone to be a leader in the Church in a way which excludes the Church itself.

From Within and Without

If a calling is truly from God, it will come through your brothers and sisters in the Church as well as within yourself. Your feeling of being called needs confirmation. You cannot really be confident in a vocation if it is based purely on your feelings, no matter how strong. When there is a real rapport between your own settled feeling and the settled feeling of others, then you can begin to be sure. A sure-safe vocation is found in a 'marriage' between a sense of a call to your heart and a call from outside yourself, from the Church community.

You will need other people to help you discover what God is asking of you. These may include your family and friends, those you work with, people at Church, your local priest, school or college chaplain, or a priest-friend. You must allow them to be really honest with you. The confirmation you need may come without you even having to ask. If people come to you and say, "I think you would make a good priest" or ask "Have you ever thought of becoming a priest?", then perhaps Jesus is calling you gently through their questions. Ask them why they think you might be suitable. The feelings and ideas of others can be truly blessed, and their thoughts may be the thoughts of the Lord.

"Lord Christ, gentle and humble of heart, we hear your timid call: 'You, follow me.' You give us this vocation so that together we may live a parable of communion and, having taken the risk of an entire lifetime, we may be ferments of reconciliation in that irreplaceable communion called the Church.
Show us how to respond courageously, without getting trapped in the quicksand of our hesitations.
Come, so that we many be sustained by the breath of your Spirit, the one thing that matters, without which nothing impels us to keep on moving forward.
You ask all who know how to love and suffer with you to leave themselves behind and follow you.
When, to love with you and not without you, we must abandon some project contrary to your plan, then come, O Christ, and fill us with quiet confidence: make us realise that your love will never disappear, and that to follow you means giving our lives."

Brother Roger of Taizé

Chapter

Initial steps: Your Bishop and Your Calling

In the end, it is your bishop who has the task of discerning your gifts and vocation. The call to the priesthood is a very special gift or charism. It is not a private blessing, but a summons to public service, in and for the Church. As the one who speaks in a special way for Jesus and his Church, your bishop will play a vital role in helping you to discover and fulfil the call of Jesus. Only when he lays hands on you at your ordination can you be fully sure that you are called to be a priest.

Through the apostles Jesus called others to share his ministry. He continues this today, through his bishops. We cannot totally separate Jesus' silent call to our hearts and the bishop's acceptance of our vocation. The bishop is in the fullest sense the living instrument of the Good Shepherd himself, and the ministry of a priest makes no sense apart from the bishop who calls a man to share his ministry. It is his confirmation above all that you will need before you can be really confident about the feeling you have.

Am I the Right Sort of Person?

You have only to join a gathering of priests anywhere, or visit a seminary, to realise that there is no such thing as a single 'priestly type'. Priests are people as varied as any other group, widely different in interests, temperament and background. This is one of the riches of the priesthood. No priest can, in practice, be all things to all people. So do not worry if you are not very much like some other priests you know. You may think you are an unlikely person to be a priest, but so do most priests. The apostles themselves were a very mixed group of people. What mattered was that Jesus chose them, and they said 'Yes'.

A True Disciple of Jesus

Anyone who is going to be a pastoral leader of the disciples of Jesus must be someone who is already a disciple – a committed Christian. There are certain signs your bishop and others will look for as they try to help you discern your calling. Do not be too worried about these, or overwhelmed by them. Like the rest of us, you are someone who fails and falls: we are all sinners (1 John 1: 8-10). What matters is that you have already steadfastly set out on your pilgrim journey, the path to holiness, with your fellow disciples. They will expect to see someone who is taking seriously his faith in Jesus Christ. These are the some of the things they will look for:
   • A real love for God, a living relationship with Jesus Christ
   • An established and developing life of prayer: you are still learning, stumbling, perhaps even struggling, but a man of prayer all the same
   • A love for the Eucharist as something really central to your life
   • A living commitment to Jesus shown by your way of life, your keeping of the commandments as a sign of your love, living a life worthy of your Christian vocation
   • An eagerness to serve Jesus in his Church, a deep and settled zeal for bringing the Good News of Jesus to others

"Look, I am standing at the door, knocking. If one of you hears me calling and opens the door, I will come in and share his meal, side by side with him"
Revelation 3. 20

- Some experience of sharing your faith with others
- Some active involvement in the worship, life and mission of your local Catholic community (parish or chaplaincy)
- A reasonable understanding of your Catholic faith, and of what it means to be a priest
- A real love for the Catholic Church: whatever criticisms you may have of it, as we all do, you should be someone who feels at home in the Church as it is, ready to serve from within
- a real personal desire to be a priest, truly free, settled and tested by time
- a readiness to offer your whole life to God's service, holding nothing back: not worrying too much about your natural worries and hesitations
- a willingness to let Jesus work through you and use you as he chooses

This is not meant to be a check-list. However, going through it will give you some idea of the kind of living faith expected in someone who is offering himself for service as a priest. Do not be concerned if your response to some of these things is "Yes, but ..." If your response is "No" in some areas, this does not mean you are not being called to the priesthood, but it may mean you are not yet ready to begin formation in a seminary.

A Good Human Being, Who Cares for Others

A priest is the human instrument of Jesus the Good Shepherd. He can only be a really good priest if he is a good human being. This means he must have certain basic human qualities. Words which come to mind are 'ordinary', 'normal', 'balanced' and 'mature'. There are all kinds of problems about defining what these mean, but there is a down-to-earth common-sense understanding of what is expected.

When people are asked about the human qualities needed in a priest, certain ones are almost always near the top of the list: he must be friendly and approachable, caring, understanding, considerate, generous, sensitive, a good listener, patient, forgiving, reliable and well-mannered. In other words, he must have a deep love for people, and be able to show that love. He has to be someone who can relate comfortably with the wide range of people who will

Picture courtesy of JOHN ROSS

"Heralds of the Gospel are needed who are experts in humanity, who have penetrated the depths of the heart of people of today, who share in their joys and hopes, their anguishes and sorrows, and who at the same time are contemplatives in love with God".
(Pope John Paul II - Address to European Bishops 1985)

be entrusted to his care as a priest. This means people of all ages, nationalities, different backgrounds, both men and women. This ability to be at ease with other people, to reach out to them and communicate with them, is absolutely essential for any priest. Your bishop will therefore look for signs that you are able to establish and sustain strong and caring relationships with others. Future priests should therefore cultivate a series of human qualities, not only out of proper and due growth and realisation of self, but also with a view to the ministry. These qualities are needed for them to be balanced people, strong and free, capable of bearing the weight of pastoral responsibilities.

A Balanced Person

The word 'balanced' is a vital one! The Church is looking for men of ordinary human maturity. What is expected depends, of course, on your age: more will be expected of you if you are 30 than if you are 18. The priesthood is a strenuous and exacting ministry. It requires reasonably good physical health, but also mental and emotional stability to cope with the stresses and strains, the burdens and demands of the priesthood. Strength of character is required, and a fair share of determination and courage, as well as a good and normal sense of humour!

Reasonable Intelligence

A teaching ministry is central to the priesthood, and a priest has to be properly equipped for preaching and teaching in many ways. The Church expects its priests to be people of reasonable intelligence, with a good basic education as a foundation. Dioceses vary as to what they require. Some academic achievement up to GCSE and A-level is the usual minimum standard for young people, but age and experience will be taken into account. The bishop will want to see that you can cope with priestly formation. What matters above all is that you will be able to grasp and faithfully pass on the Good News and the Church's teaching.

Openness and Freedom Within

It is not just intelligence that matters. You must be someone who is willing to be formed for the priesthood, and able to be formed. This calls for an inner flexibility, and openness to change and renewal. It requires true self-discipline and a sense of responsibility. It also demands the right motivation, and real freedom of heart. You must be free enough to say a true "Yes" to God's call, and to take on a ministry which will ask much of you – a freely-given lifetime commitment to a celibate way of loving, obedient service with your bishop and his priests, and a simple lifestyle of joyful sacrifice.

"Since, as president, he will be God's representative, he must be irreproachable: never an arrogant or hot-tempered man, nor a heavy drinker or violent, not out to make money; but a man who is hospitable and a friend of all that is good: sensible, moral, devout and self-controlled, so that he can be counted on for both expounding the sound doctrine and refuting those who argue against it." (Titus 1: 7-9)

"Here is a saying that you can rely on: to want to be a presiding elder is to want to do a noble work. That is why the president must have an impeccable character." (1 Timothy 3: 1)

The qualities asked of a good priest are much the same as for a good husband and father, and the perfect priest is as elusive as the perfect husband! The Church is just as choosy about its priests as a bride is about a prospective husband. The human qualities needed in a priest or in a husband are much the same: freedom, maturity, lifelong commitment, sacrificial self-giving, compatibility and above all, a true and deep love. No one is perfect, but both bride and Church know in their heart-of-hearts the degree that is required.

Who then is a suitable candidate for priestly formation? An unmarried Catholic man, who is an ordinary, balanced person, with a maturity appropriate for his age and experience, of reasonable health and intelligence, able to make a free choice for his future, a loving and caring person who relates easily with other people, and a true disciple and friend of Jesus Christ, already living out in the Church the vocation he has from his Baptism and Confirmation. And, of course, he must also feel called to priesthood.

How Old?

You will have to be at least 18 before you enter one of our major seminaries, and usually 25 before you are ordained a priest. In their Charter for Priestly Formation, the bishops of England and Wales state that recent converts should not normally go to a seminary until at least three years after their reception into the Church. This does not mean that a teenager or recent convert cannot begin looking seriously at a possible call to the priesthood and laying the foundations for future formation.

There is no set upper-age limit, so older men can be accepted too; however, common-sense dictates that anyone applying for ministry must be able to give a good number of years' service as a priest after the years he has spent in seminary. It is therefore unlikely that a bishop would accept candidates who are coming up to retirement in their 60s.

Chapter

8

What do I do next?

Give It Time

You may be young or not so young. You may be involved with studies, or working, or unemployed. Perhaps you have recently been received into full communion with the Catholic Church, or you have had a deep religious experience and feel God has entered your life in a special way.

Something deep inside you suggests that Jesus may be calling you to be a priest. You are not sure why, and you have all kinds of doubts and worries about the whole idea. Discovering your true vocation is rather like falling in love; you will go through a whole range of emotions, ups and downs, moments of commitment and moments of hesitation. The whole seminary experience itself will be a journey of discovery, a time of discernment and that, at the moment, lies in the future. Do not make a decision in a hurry. Be patient with yourself and with those who are trying to help and advise you. Give yourself time to reflect and discuss.

What follows in this chapter is a number of suggestions that many men have found helpful in the first stages of their vocational discernment. They are suggested as pointers rather than demands or requirements. You might find that you are able to do some, but not all of them. Everyone is different and so there is no magical recipe for success.

Stay Close to the Lord and to Others

Make sure that during this time you stay close to the Lord you seek to follow. Let him be your companion on the way you are journeying. Your family and friends can also be a real support at this time. Even if they are not happy with the idea of you becoming a priest, do not cut yourself off from them. You will also need the support of your local parish community or chaplaincy. As people who know you and care about you, they can help you in the whole process of finding your future.

Prayer

Your personal relationship with Jesus is the heart of any vocation you have from him. It is above all in your prayer that you will hear his voice and know the spiritual calm that comes from discovering his will of love for you.

Deepen your prayer-life as you test your vocation. Try different kinds of prayer, read books on prayer, join other people in prayer. The Divine Office, the Prayer of the Church, will be an important part of your ministry if you become a priest: perhaps begin now to pray part of it each day (eg, morning and evening prayer).

Ask God to show you what he wants of you, and to guide those who are there to help you and to discern your vocation. Ask others to pray for you. Become more and more a man of prayer.

Make the Eucharist central to your life. Sunday Mass should be the climax of your week, but it may be possible for you to go to Mass on other days as well. Grow to love the Eucharist, spend time in adoration of the Blessed Sacrament and become a truly Eucharistic person.

A priest is a minister of reconciliation, a man of God's forgiveness. The Sacrament of Reconciliation (Confession) should be important to you, difficult though it sometimes is. Perhaps find a priest that you can go to regularly and openly. You may like to ask him or someone else to be your 'spiritual director' or helper during this time of waiting and testing. You can talk to him or her openly about your feelings and your developing sense of a vocation. Many people do in fact opt to find a spiritual director to help them on their journey. A spiritual director is an experienced guide in matters of faith and prayer. This would normally be a priest or religious who is accountable to the Church. The spiritual director would meet with their directee for an hour or so, perhaps each month, to discuss prayer and life generally.

> "Some dioceses recommend that each enquirer for priesthood has a spiritual director... normally a priest would be recommended"

Some dioceses recommend that each enquirer for priesthood has a spiritual director (in addition to the vocations director who deals with the discernment and selection process). As spiritual direction is often linked to the Sacrament of Reconciliation, normally a priest would be recommended. If choosing one's own spiritual director, it would be important to remember what spiritual direction is about – it is about being probed and challenged as well as being supported and guided. Therefore, while it might be valid to choose someone with whom you naturally feel comfortable, this 'soul-mate' should also be someone who is impartial and not afraid of asking difficult questions and giving sometimes unwelcome advice.

It would be good also to make use of days of reflection and retreats organised locally, or by your diocese, or perhaps by a religious community. Some of these are specially focused on the whole idea of God's calling and your personal choices for your future.

Talk with Other People

Do not tell everyone you want to be a priest, or that you are thinking about it. Sometimes this can make it more difficult for you to make a free decision. People's hopes and expectations can put much pressure on you. Your vocation must come from Jesus himself, not from your mother or father, your parish priest or your favourite religious brother or sister.

But do talk to some people you trust. Ask them to be really honest with you about your strengths and weaknesses. Do they see you as a priest? Their response can be an important way in which Jesus himself confirms his call to you.

Talk to people who know the priesthood from the inside. If you have the chance, get to know a few priests. This will bring you down-to-earth in your understanding of the kind of people Jesus calls to the priesthood, but also give you some rich insights into what it really means to be a priest. Keep in touch with a priest you can relate to easily.

Find Out More

The very fact that you are reading this book probably suggests that you are keen to discover more about the priesthood and what it involves.

Spend time doing some further reading and reflection. Read the Scriptures regularly. A prayerful reading of St Luke's Gospel, for example, will give you a rich vision both of your calling as a Christian and of what sharing Jesus' ministry in a special way will involve.

Read some basic introductions to the Catholic Faith so that you have a sound knowledge of who Jesus is and what he has done for us. Search for more understanding about what the Church is and what it is for. Perhaps a deeper appreciation of the meaning of the Sacraments would be helpful. Read about the priestly ministry. What you read will depend on who you are and the stage you have reached on your journey of faith. A good starting place to learn about all the above is 'The Catechism of the Catholic Church' or the abridged version of it.

Get Involved

Become as involved as you sensibly can in your local Church community, in its worship, its work to spread the Good News, its care for those in need, and in its community life. If you are already an altar server, see this as a special ministry of service. Offer yourself as a Reader at Mass; in this way you are a bearer of God's Word to his people. If you are asked to be an extra-ordinary minister of Holy Communion accept this honour gladly. There may be other ways of helping with the Liturgy: helping in the sacristy, getting involved with music at Mass, joining in the welcoming ministry.

It is also important to share in the apostolic work of the parish or chaplaincy, and its care for others. You may be able to help as a catechist, preparing people

Listen to the call: Talk to your local vocation director about your calling

Picture courtesy of JOHN ROSS

for the Sacraments and in other ways. Perhaps there is a special children's liturgy at a Sunday Mass in your church, or people are needed to help with classes for children in non-Catholic schools. Get involved also in activities which show your love for people, especially those in need. The Saint Vincent de Paul Group will need support and the Justice and Peace Group will welcome fresh enthusiasm. Perhaps you could even brave the parish Youth Club and offer your services.

Obviously you cannot do all these things, nor should you. But it would be good if you could find at least one main way of being involved in both the worship and the witness of your local Church. This will deepen your personal Christian commitment, and it will also help you and others to see what kind of ministry you are suited to in the Church.

Make Contact with the Diocesan Vocations Director for Priesthood

Every diocese has a priest in it who is nominated by the bishop to help him deal with those who may feel called to priesthood. The Vocations Director has two main roles: to help people with initial discernment and to help them with their application for priesthood. The Vocation Director is there to help, so don't be afraid to make contact with him. Contact details for each diocesan Vocations Director are available on the Internet at www.ukpriest.org, or by asking your local priest.

The Vocations Director will give you information, guidance and advice. Each diocese varies as to what activities are organised. You may find you are invited to join a group of others exploring their vocation; such a group may meet regularly for reflection, prayer and social events. Some dioceses organize vocation days and weekends, or longer retreats. These can be a real help in focusing yourself on the question at hand: is Jesus calling you to be his priest?

Normally, if you were seriously interested in the priesthood you would meet with the Vocations Director, fairly informally at first, to discuss how you feel. If initial signs are encouraging, meetings might then take place on a more formal footing so that both of you have the opportunity to discuss important issues. You should understand that these initial discussions are without any obligation from either side, just an exploration of where your life is going and what you are experiencing.

Eventually, if both you and the Vocations Director feel you might genuinely have a vocation to the priesthood, then you would be encouraged to make a formal application to the bishop. This would then involve actively participating in the Church's selection process for priesthood. This process is there to help the bishop (and his advisors) make an initial judgement about a man's suitability for priestly formation.

> "Lord show me clearly what you want me to do with the gifts you have given me.
> Grant me the strength that I need to answer your call with courage and love.
> Make me a generous person so that others may experience your love through me.
> Help me always to look to You as the One who will show me the way to live my life"
> Amen

Chapter

How Do I Apply?
The Selection Process

What is Selection?

When someone feels called by God to become a priest it is important that they have plenty of time to think and pray about this so that they and others can discern whether in fact this is their true vocation.

Beginning formation for the priesthood is a big step. Those who are in formation already will have had to give up their jobs and maybe even their homes. Also, being a priest is quite challenging and therefore it is important that those who apply for the priesthood are properly assessed before they are accepted.

The diocesan selection process aims to help the bishop to make a preliminary assessment about a candidate who presents himself for priesthood. The bishop must judge whether or not the candidate may be hearing a call from God to priesthood, and whether that candidate will be able to meet the demands of both priestly formation and life as a priest in today's world.

Picture courtesy of JOHN ROSS

"You and other potential candidates for priestly formation may be invited to a seminary to meet the staff and students and get a taste of seminary life..."

Who Decides Whether I am to be Selected or Not?

It is the bishop who makes the final decision about whether a candidate is accepted or not. He will seek the advice of others before he makes that decision, including those who know the candidate well and those who would be involved in preparing the candidate for ordination.

The diocesan vocations director is specially appointed by the diocesan bishop to help him in the selection of candidates for the priesthood. The vocations director is an experienced priest and he will be your primary point of reference throughout the selection process. He is there to help and advise you at every stage.

Pope Benedict XVI, in one of his homilies written before he was Pope said:

"There is no right to the priesthood. One cannot choose it as one chooses this job or that. One can only be chosen for it - by him. To be a priest does not belong to the list of human rights, and no one can sue to obtain it." **('Ministers of Your Joy' 1988).**

The Catechism of the Catholic Church says of those aspiring to the priesthood:

"No one has a right to receive the sacrament of Holy Orders. Indeed no one claims this office for himself - he is called to it by God. Anyone who thinks he recognises the signs of God's call to the ordained ministry must humbly submit his desire to the authority of the Church who has the responsibility and right to call someone to receive orders." *(Catechism of the Catholic Church, paragraph 1578).*

It is the bishop who has the responsibility and right to do this in his own diocese, and he does this with the help of the selection process.

The Selection Process

If you decide that you are still interested in the priesthood, and you have a strong sense of God calling you to be a priest, then it is time to apply to take part in the selection process. This takes quite a while, but it is important not to rush anything. The process is there to help discern what God is asking of you. Whatever happens in the end, you will learn a lot about yourself and you will be closer to discovering what Jesus is calling you to do for him.

The following is a list of the various components that make up the diocesan selection process. You will be asked to take part in most, if not all of these. It is also possible that the bishop may ask for other things to be included as part of the selection process. The vocations director will know what is required and will advise you at every stage.

Throughout the selection process, the vocations director will try to be as open as possible with you and keep you informed about how you are getting on, but you should understand that he does not have the final say in your selection and also that he may be bound by confidentiality on some issues.

Meetings with the vocations director

Once you meet the vocations director you should be in touch with one another on a regular basis so that he can help in the discernment of your vocation and also guide you through the selection process.

Selection Advisory Conference

You and other potential candidates for priestly formation may be invited to a seminary to meet the staff and students and also to get a taste of seminary life. This is normally a weekend visit, which incorporates interviews with members of seminary staff and others who will prepare a report for the bishop based on how they feel you would get on at seminary. For this weekend you will have to fill in an application form, which the vocations director will provide and also you might be asked to write an essay along the lines of why priesthood is of interest to you. The vocations director will also let you know if anything else will be required of you.

Medical Examination

You will be asked to go to your doctor for a general medical examination, the results of which will be made available to doctors who are on the bishop's selection advisory panel.

Psychological Assessment

A fully trained psychologist who has a good knowledge of the Catholic priesthood will undertake a psychological assessment with you. The aim of the assessment is to help you to understand the factors at work in your life and the implications of these for vocational effectiveness. It may also indicate areas of potential growth in the future.

At the end of the assessment the psychologist will present you with a personal report which you will be able to discuss with them. You will also share these confidential findings with the vocations director and the bishop.

References

You will be asked to provide the names of a number of referees, one of whom should normally be your parish priest or chaplain. The bishop may also approach other people whom he feels can offer relevant advice. In common with other caring professions, appropriate checks are made on those who apply for the priesthood; this will include a criminal record check.

*What's it like?: Potential candidates are invited
to meet staff and get a taste of seminary life*
Picture courtesy of JOHN ROSS

Proof of Baptism and Confirmation (or reception)

You will be asked to write to the parish where you were baptised, asking the priest of that place to provide you with certification of your baptism and confirmation in the Catholic community. If you were not originally baptised in the Catholic community, but we received into it at a later date, it is the parish where the reception took place that would be contacted.

Interview with the bishop and his advisory panel

Finally, all the above will be taken into account at a formal interview with the bishop and his advisory panel, if he has one. Some time after this interview you will be informed as to whether or not the bishop has accepted you for priestly formation. The vocations director will inform you of the bishop's decision as soon as he can.

What if I am Selected?

If selected you would normally begin formation for the priesthood either at a seminary or some other place (such as a parish in the diocese) at the start of the academic year.

What if I am not Selected?

It is important to appreciate that applying for the priesthood is not the same as applying for a job. If you are not accepted it does not mean that you have 'failed' – it simply means that perhaps your real vocation lies elsewhere. The vocations director will provide what help he can if you are not accepted.

While all of the above may seem somewhat daunting please do not be unduly worried about it. Please remember that the process is there to establish what God wants of you and what is in the best interests of both yourself and the Church. Therefore, please do not view the selection process as a series of 'job interviews', but rather as part of your vocational discernment.

Every morning in the Divine Office, the Prayer of the Church, the priest prays the Benedictus, the song of Zechariah (Luke 1. 68-79). These words spoken of the prophet John the Baptist sum up much of the priest's own ministry:

You shall be called a prophet of God the Most High.
You shall go ahead of the Lord
to prepare his ways before him,
to make known to people their salvation
through forgiveness of all their sins,
the loving kindness of the heart of our God
who visits us like the dawn from on high.
He will give light to those in darkness,
those who dwell in the shadow of death,
and guide us into the way of peace

(Grail version)

Formation for Priesthood

How are Priests Trained?

The apostles spent three years close to Jesus, preparing for when they would be sent out in his name. They spent time with him, they were taught by him, and they were formed into a small community centred on him. Today the Church uses special places of formation called seminaries to prepare men for priesthood. The purpose of the years at the seminary is to relive, in a way, the experience of the 12 apostles. If you are accepted for priestly formation, you are likely to be in a seminary for up to six years, (although account will be taken of your age and experience). There you will spend time in prayer, you will study, you will gain experience in various pastoral situations and you will be part of a community.

A seminary is a residential college run by the Church where students and staff (both priests and lay people) live together in a community of faith. During his time in the seminary, each student tries to discover God's will for him, and whether Jesus is calling him to be a priest. The purpose of the formation in seminary is not simply to train someone to do priestly things, but to form the whole person and also to enable the student and his local bishop to make a mature decision as to whether priesthood is for him.

Our Seminaries

The dioceses of England and Wales have several seminaries for preparing men for priesthood, and not all of these are in this country. During parts of the 16th and 17th Centuries, a time of great religious and political upheaval, it was illegal to be a Catholic priest or to attend Mass. Because of this persecution, it was necessary for priestly formation to take place in other parts of Europe, and so colleges were established in places such as Valladolid (Spain), Rome and Douai. Even when it became possible to prepare men for priesthood in this country once again, some of the colleges abroad were kept and are still doing their work today, some 400 years later.

Today, we have seminaries in Rome, (the Venerable English and Welsh College and the Beda College), in Durham (Ushaw), in Birmingham (Oscott), in London (Allen Hall) and near Guildford, (Wonersh). The college at Valladolid in Spain plays a distinctive role today in preparing candidates for life in the other seminaries, perhaps by helping them to understand their faith in more depth or by assisting them in the development of their academic skills or spirituality. Each of the seminaries has its own website and these are well worth visiting.

Life In Seminary

Although priestly formation in the seminary is viewed holistically as a single experience, it can be broken down into the four main areas listed below:

Liturgy and Prayer

The apostles asked Jesus to teach them to pray, and were often with him when he prayed. Anyone preparing for ministry must become, above all, a man of prayer. Daily Mass is the centre of community life, and celebrating the official prayer of the Church (The Divine Office) together is an important part of each day. Prayer groups of various kinds exist in all seminaries.

The student has to develop his own distinctive prayer life, and it is vital that he spends some time each day in private prayer. Every seminary organises Days of Recollection and longer retreats during the course of each year. Each student also has a 'spiritual director' who helps him respond to God and to discern his vocation, as well as watching over his growing prayer life and overall spiritual development.

Study

The apostles were taught by Jesus, and they in their turn went out to teach others. As St Paul put it: "This is what I received from the Lord, and in turn passed on to you" (1 Corinthians 11.23). A considerable amount of time is spent at the seminary studying. There are courses in the Scriptures, the Church's teaching on doctrine and morality, Liturgy, Church History, Canon Law and Philosophy, as well as courses which help students to more fully understand the society in which they will serve. Many of these are explained on the seminaries' websites.

The seminaries have links with universities at home or overseas. Some students may take courses which lead to a degree in theology. Courses are very flexible however, and account is taken of the individual experience, needs and abilities of each student.

The student is preparing for a ministry of serving, teaching and preaching. He can only give straightforward instruction, counsel and advice if he has a deep well of knowledge from which to draw.

Pastoral Experience

The apostles and the 72 disciples were sent out by Jesus during their three years with him (Luke 9:1-6; 10:1-10). The same happens to those preparing for the apostolic ministry today. From the beginning of their formation, students are sent out for various pastoral experiences so that they can develop pastoral skills and learn a great deal about themselves and the priestly ministry.

Pastoral experience, (which is a bit like 'work experience' in schools), would include visiting the elderly and the sick, at home or in hospital. There would also be opportunities to spend time in primary and secondary schools, in youth groups, in prisons, and with the disabled. Parish pastoral visiting, calling from house to house and developing the vital ministry of presence of being with people, would also be available. Once or twice a year students may spend an extended period of several weeks or a month in a parish or other pastoral placements.

For many students their formation now includes a pastoral placement of about six months to a year, somewhere in the middle of their training. The student is very much like a lay pastoral assistant during this time, and it can be a very important experience for seeing whether he can cope with an eventual role as a pastoral leader in a parish. Pastoral training in the seminary also includes work in preaching, counselling, spiritual direction and catechetics.

Human Formation

A priest is a public figure and people must have confidence in him. He must also have confidence in himself. It is important that those who will serve as priests be rounded, balanced individuals who know what their gifts, talents and weaknesses are. No one would expect someone who had just entered seminary to be good at everything. One of the opportunities that seminaries provide is space and time for growth as a person. Living in community with others helps with this. If there are particular issues that an individual needs help with (for example having the confidence to stand up to speak in front of others) then this is all part of seminary formation.

A priest also needs to commit himself to the specific demands of priesthood, including promises of celibacy and obedience. It is important for someone preparing for priesthood to spend time coming to a mature understanding of these.

A Day in the Seminary

Most seminaries have a regular daily timetable which encompasses the various aspects of formation within a community context. Typically, a day would start before 8am with morning prayer or Mass. After breakfast, a series of lectures or seminars would follow, with some students attending a local university for these. After lunch there would normally be time for pastoral work, spiritual direction, sport or study. After an evening meal, seminarians might attend prayer groups or spend time in each other's company, relaxing and chatting.

At weekend, the timetable would be slightly different as students normally get a day off, and on Sunday the Eucharist takes pride of place. Some students might also help in local parishes at weekends.

Testing time: Life in seminary has light-hearted moments but overall is a thorough examination of your suitability to the priesthood

A Demanding Experience

The three years the apostles spent with Jesus were far from easy, and the same is true of seminary life. Jesus does not promise a cosy, comfortable life, but renouncing oneself, taking up the cross and following in his footsteps. The time spent in seminary formation is as vital for today's aspirants to priesthood as were those years spent with Jesus by the apostles.

Seminary life is certainly a testing time, a challenging and demanding experience. Only if it is so can formation really help to prepare a man for the tremendous ministry of the priesthood. If you read a Gospel account of how the apostles were formed by Jesus, you will have some idea of what to expect in the seminary. It will, of course, be very different to that small band wandering round Galilee with their Master.

Times are different, and there are new demands and needs. But the heart of it all is the same: Jesus forming a group of special friends to share his own ministry, and forming them in the ways of radical discipleship and total commitment to him.

'Seminary life is certainly a testing time, a challenging and demanding experience... only if it is so can formation really help to prepare a man for the priesthood'

Key Moments In The Seminary

During his time of preparation, the seminarian reaches various 'milestones' on his journey to the priesthood:

• At some stage, well into his formation programme, **he will be accepted as a Candidate for Holy Orders.** For the first time he publicly proclaims his desire to be a priest and his commitment to continue his formation. The bishop receives him as one he hopes will persevere in his training and become a priest.

• **He will receive the Ministry of Reader.** Although a lay ministry, this will also remind him of his need to prepare for the priest's task of proclaiming the Gospel

• **He will receive the lay Ministry of Acolyte,** looking ahead to the priest's role in the Eucharist and the other sacraments.

• Towards the end of his time at the seminary **he will be ordained as a deacon.** He may now baptise, preach, preside at weddings and funerals, and lead the people in prayer. He commits himself to life-long celibacy and to praying the Divine Office. The new deacon will exercise his ministry either in the seminary or in a parish.

"I offer you, Lord, my thoughts, to be fixed on you;
my words, to have you for their theme;
my actions, to be done according to your will;
my hardships, to be endured for your sake.
My will is that your will be done, in the manner you will, and as long as you will, because it is your will."

Prayer ascribed to Pope Clement XI

To Young People...

An extract from a communique by the Synod of Bishops in 1990

"We would like to say a word to you young people, the hope of the Church. We recognise your generosity and idealism, and ask you to reflect with us on the vocation to the priesthood. A priestly vocation comes from God, a gift which he offers to young men whom he trusts to imitate Jesus Christ in serving God and humanity.

We can promise you, from our experience, that it is worthwhile to give one's life and strength as a priest in the service of the people of God. In spite of each difficulty, such a life can always bring joy and happiness. Jesus Christ himself has promised us that 'he who loses his life for my sake will find it.'

The Church and the world need good shepherds, priests ready to serve God and the people of God with free hearts and free hands. We know that it is not easy to answer God's call to priesthood. But we trust, dear brothers, that with God's help many young men will answer such a call.

During the discussions in the Synod we have heard welcome news that priestly vocations in some countries are numerous, while other countries experience a growing shortage of priests. It is clear many young people find it hard to commit themselves to lifelong priesthood, to give up the possibility of marriage and setting up a family, and to choose a life in the spirit of the evangelical counsels, of poverty, chastity and obedience.

But priests should be free from ties of marriage and family, not attached to possessions and comfort, not demanding complete personal autonomy. This is a high ideal. Yet in every age, including our own, we have seen marvellous examples of their heroism, with some even suffering martyrdom for their vocation.

Therefore we ask you, young people, with your parishes, to pray with us that the Lord of the harvest send labourers to the harvest. The entire people of God needs priests. So we hope and pray that your families, your friends and your communities come to understand the importance of the call to priesthood, and better support those of you who choose this path."

Chapter

11

You are a Priest Forever: Ordination and beyond

Final Steps Before Ordination

Once a trainee priest has undertaken five years of formation in seminary, and also has spent time working in pastoral situations, an important decision has to be made: this is the decision as to whether that person should now be ordained. A number of important considerations need to be taken into account, such as how the individual has coped during formation, how he relates to the people he will be serve, whether or not he will be able to adequately fulfil the demands of life as a priest, and most importantly, does this man really have a good sense of being called by God to serve as a priest?

If the candidate wishes to proceed to ordination, at this stage he makes a formal application to his bishop. Note that throughout the years of formation the candidate is discerning his vocation – if he felt at any time that priesthood was not his true vocation then he could have left the seminary without further obligation. He must be free in his vocational choices and no pressure would have been put on him. Once he has been ordained, however, there is no turning back; the obligations of ordained ministry are part of his life.

Diaconate

There are a number of steps throughout priestly formation that direct the path to ordination. During time in seminary, a seminarian would be formally accepted as a candidate and would also be instituted into the ministries of acolyte and reader (see previous chapter). One final step before becoming a priest is ordination as a deacon. The diaconate is an ordained ministry in its own right, which involves preaching the gospel and also assisting at the altar. A deacon has the authority to baptise and to marry, but he cannot preside like a priest at Mass or hear confessions. Once a man has become a deacon, the obligations of celibacy, obedience and daily praying of the Divine Office become part of his life.

Priestly Ordination

Normally a man who was aspiring to priesthood would be a deacon for six months to a year, and then the bishop would ordain him as priest. The ordination of a priest is an important day in the life of the Church community and the ceremony would normally be attended by many people including family, friends and other priests.

The rite of ordination has a number of important parts to it. Each part is like a little ceremony within the whole service, which is always a Mass with a bishop presiding. The parts of the rite of ordination are as follows:

• The people of God affirm that the man to be ordained has been found worthy of ordination, and the bishop solemnly chooses him to be a priest. He affirms his resolve to undertake the priestly ministry, and promises continued respect and obedience to the bishop and his successors.

• Then he prostrates himself on the floor as a sign that he is giving his 'all' to the Lord. The people ask the saints to pray for him.

• The bishop lays his hands on the man's head in silence, an ancient symbol of the coming of the Holy Spirit; the Spirit of power and love, of authority and of service. All the other priests present come forward, silently laying their hands upon him. The bishop now says the solemn prayer of consecration asking God to grant him the dignity of the priesthood. The man is now a priest, a co-worker with the bishop and his brother priests. The laying-on of hands by the bishop puts the new priest in touch with the ministers of the Church right back to the apostles themselves. He now shares their special ministry, which is the ministry of Christ himself.

Ordination day: *A joyous occasion for both you and your family*

• Next the new priest is clothed in his priestly vestments, including a stole and chasuble.

• The bishop anoints the new priest's hands with the oil of Chrism, asking Jesus to preserve him to sanctify God's people and to offer sacrifice to God.

• He is presented with the paten and chalice for the Eucharist, with the prayer that he will model his whole life on the mystery he will celebrate.

• The bishop and the other priests present give him the sign of peace, a gesture of welcome and of brotherly love.

Then, for the first time, he concelebrates the Eucharist with the bishop and priests – now, and for the rest of his life, as priest of Jesus Christ.

After Ordination: The First Appointment

Once a priest has been ordained, the bishop will normally appoint him to his first parish. Here he will serve God and his people, together with an experienced priest whose task it will be to help and guide him in those first few, all-important, months.

It will be necessary for a new priest to establish a routine, based on the needs of the parish he is living in. The first few days will normally involve meeting many of the people in the community and getting used to the locality. It is unlikely, however, that he will enjoy a gradual easing-in to the priestly life; rather he will be expected to take an active role from day one. After all, the needs of the people aren't going to go away for the convenience of him settling in!

It is at this point that all those years spent in formation really begin to bear fruit. There is an extent to which the 'theory' learned in seminary will now be put into practice; however, even during his training he will have spent time in parishes, so it won't all be completely new. It would also be true to say that the seminary didn't teach the new priest everything – it would be impossible to cover every eventuality and circumstance. Therefore, there is a lot of learning still to be done. The parish priest he is serving with, and other colleagues too, will only be too happy to offer help and advice.

As time progresses, some of the things that seemed strange or difficult at first will become second-nature. The time and effort invested into developing good relationships with others will pay-off. New friendships will be formed and trust be built. The rhythm of parish life with its the liturgical seasons, the people he meets daily and the tasks he does, will soon begin to shape the priest. He will grow in confidence and become a really valued member of the local community, not so much because of what he does, rather because of what he is – a priest of Jesus Christ.

On-going Formation and Support

Priestly formation in seminary has led the new priest to this point, but it does not end here. Formation continues for the rest of priestly life and ministry, as Jesus himself seeks to deepen and enrich service of him and his flock. Of course we all learn from experience, but sometimes it is important to reflect on that experience or to learn new things. Many dioceses provide training days for their clergy throughout the year, and sometimes a priest might be asked by his bishop to undertake further studies in specialist areas.

Jesus often went into the hills or a lonely place to pray. A priest normally has the opportunity of making a spiritual retreat during the year, perhaps quietly on his own or alternatively with colleagues on a planned retreat with input from speakers.

> "The clergy of a deanery will meet several times a year... sometimes just for discussion and friendship It is important that a new priest gets good support from the clergy of his diocese"

As dioceses are often quite large, they are split into deaneries. A deanery is a cluster of parishes, conveniently arranged, based on geographic location. Normally the clergy of a deanery would meet several times a year for ongoing training, or sometimes just for discussion and fellowship.

Although a priest will remain in contact with family and friends, it will be necessary to develop healthy relationships with others, too. Many of those who were in seminary with a priest will become ordained colleagues and will stay in contact with him. It will also be important that a new priest gets good support from the clergy of his diocese, especially those ordained fairly recently. Many dioceses provide opportunities for those ordained for up to five or ten years to meet periodically.

A priest's friends and associates do not all have to be priests. Many lay people will also be in a priest's social circle. However, a priest cannot be everyone's

Picture courtesy of JOHN ROSS

friend and nor can he relate to everyone in exactly the same way. While he should be generally friendly to others, often his relationship will be that of pastor, not pal, and so he must remember where the boundaries in his life and ministry are, even if these are different to the people who surround him.

It would be disingenuous to suggest that every day in a priest's life is wonderful and cheery. Like anyone else, a priest can be influenced by his moods and experiences, and like anyone else he can have 'off-days'. What is important is that a priest tries, like any other professional person, not to let his personal preferences and temperament affect his mission in a detrimental way. Sometimes things will be hard, and other times easy; sometimes joyful, other times sad – this is part of being human, not just being a priest. Like anyone else, a priest must find mature ways of handling the situations that life throws up. He is not Superman, and needs the support and help of others.

Normally a priest would carry on in active ministry until he was 75, or until he was prevented from doing so by ill health or other reason. During this time it is likely that he, and also his friends and community, would have the joy of celebrating important jubilees. These occasions provide great opportunities to celebrate all the good things that a priest has done in his ministry, and more importantly, to remember that ultimately the priesthood is Christ's, and that it begins and ends in him.

Appendices

A Way of Prayer:
Lectio Divina

Prayer is an important part of discerning a life vocation. In prayer we commune with God, praising him, listening to him and maybe asking him to help us with our needs or the needs of others. There are many different forms of prayer, all of which are valuable. One kind of prayer that many have found useful in vocational discernment is *lectio divina*, which is a particularly meditative way of praying.

Lectio divina is a slow, contemplative praying of the Scriptures. When praying this way we should try to imitate the prophet Elijah, able to listen for the "still, small voice of God" (1 Kings 19:12) knowing that we must 'hear' the voice of God, which often speaks very softly. In order to hear someone speaking softly we must learn to be silent. We must learn to love silence. If we are constantly speaking or if we are surrounded with noise, we cannot hear gentle sounds. The practice of *lectio divina*, therefore, requires that we first quiet down in order to hear God's word to us.

The selection and reading of a scriptural text is the first step in *lectio divina*. It is very different from the speed reading which modern Christians apply to newspapers, books and even to the Bible. We need to read slowly, attentively, gently listening to hear a word or phrase that is God's word for us this day.

Once a word or a passage in the Scriptures that speaks to us in a personal way has been found, we must take it in and reflect on it over minutes rather than seconds. We have the example of the Virgin Mary "pondering in her heart" what she saw and heard of Christ (Luke 2:19).

Next comes prayer – a dialogue with God; a loving conversation with the one who has invited us into his embrace. In prayer we allow the word that we have taken in, and on which we are pondering, to touch and change our deepest selves. God invites us to hold up our joys, thoughts and even our most difficult and pain-filled experiences to him.

Finally, we rest in the presence of the one who has used his word as a means of touching our lives. No one who has ever been in love needs to be reminded that there are moments in loving relationships when words are unnecessary. It is the same in our relationship with God. Once again we practice silence, letting go of our own words; instead simply enjoying the experience of being in the presence of God. Try it.

• Chose a text of the Scriptures that you wish to pray. It makes no difference which text is chosen, as long as one has no set goal of covering a certain amount of text: the amount of text 'covered' is in God's hands, not yours. You might like to choose a vocational story from the Bible, perhaps one of those listed in Chapter 1 of this book,

• Place yourself in a comfortable position and allow yourself to become silent. Focus for a few moments on your breathing; perhaps using a repetitive prayer phrase to centre yourself in prayer.

• Look at the text and read it slowly, gently. Dwell on each sentence or phrase of the reading, constantly listening for the 'still, small voice' of a word or phrase that might be for you today.

• Take the word or phrase into yourself. Memorize it and slowly repeat it to yourself, allowing it to interact with your inner world of concerns, memories and ideas. Do not be afraid of 'distractions.' Memories or thoughts are simply parts of yourself which, when they rise up during *lectio divina*, are asking to be given to God along with the rest of your inner self.

• Then speak to God. Whether you use words or ideas or images or all three is not important. Interact with God as you would with one who you know loves and accepts you. And offer to him what you have discovered in yourself during your experience in reflection.

• Finally, simply rest in God's presence and be alone with him.

"To live in the midst of the world without desiring its pleasures; to be a member of each family, yet belonging to none; to share all sufferings, to penetrate all secrets, to heal all wounds; to go from people to God and offer him their prayers; to return from God to people, to bring pardon, peace and hope, to have a heart of fire for charity, and a heart of bronze for chastity; to teach and to pardon, to console and to bless always: – this life is yours, O priest of Jesus Christ."
Jean-Baptiste Lacordaire, 1802-1861

How did others respond to their calling? Here we look at five famous figures from the Bible, and see how they responded to their calling. After each Biblical quotation there is an explanation of the events and a suggestion as to how you might interpret these Bible stories to your own life and calling.

Reflection 1: The Call of Moses (Exodus 3:1-6)

Here God is called 'Yahweh', the mysterious name he later reveals to Moses. We use the first part of it, 'Yah', at the end of 'Alleluia', which is the Hebrew for 'Praise (Hallel) to God (Yah).

> *Moses was looking after the flock of Jethro, his father-in-law, priest of Midian. He led his flock to the far side of the wilderness and came to Horeb, the mountain of God. There the angel of Yahweh appeared to him in the shape of a flame of fire, coming from the middle of a bush. Moses looked; there was the bush blazing but it was not being burnt up. "I must go and look at this strange sight,' Moses said, 'and see why the bush is not burnt.'*
> *Now Yahweh saw him go forward to look, and God called to him from the middle of the bush. 'Moses, Moses,' he said. 'Here I am,' he answered. 'Come no nearer,' he said. 'Take off your shoes, for the place on which you stand is holy ground. I am the God of your fathers,' he said, 'the God of Abraham, the God of Isaac and the God of Jacob." At this Moses covered his face, afraid to look at God.*

• Moses does not seem to have been looking for God, but God made himself known to him all the same. He comes to him in his ordinary life, looking after the flock of Jethro. He is there with you in your life now, drawing you to himself.

• You are unlikely to see a burning bush, but the eternal fire of the Holy Spirit is present all around you, and within you.

• God calls you by name, from the middle of your daily life. Whether you are in church, at home or elsewhere, you are on holy ground, made holy by the majestic love of the God of your ancestors. Take off the shoes of your heart, as it were, and adore the living God. And as you hear him call your name, say with all that you have and are, 'here I am.'

• Perhaps continue the story in your Bible to chapter 4, verse 17. We see how reluctant Moses was to take up God's call. He tried every excuse there was: 'Who am I to do this?' (cf Exodus 3.11) and 'Send someone else' (cf Exodus 3.13). Do not worry if you are just as hesitant and reluctant. It is what you do in the end that matters (cf Matthew 21.28f).

• Already as a Christian anointed with the Spirit, you are called to be a 'burning bush' for others. The whole of the priest's ministry is to be a special kind of 'burning bush'. The fire of God's presence will blaze within you without burning or destroying you, and God will speak to others and reach out to them from the midst of your life and work. Open your life in prayer to the fire of God's love.

Reflection 2: The Call of Samuel (1 Samuel 3:1-10)

Now the boy Samuel was ministering to Yahweh in the presence of Eli. It was rare for Yahweh to speak in those days; visions were uncommon. One day it happened that Eli was lying down in his room. His eyes were beginning to grow dim; he could no longer see. The lamp of God had not yet gone out, and Samuel was lying in the sanctuary of Yahweh where the ark of God was, when Yahweh called 'Samuel, Samuel'. He answered, 'Here I am'. Then he ran to Eli and said, 'Here I am, since you called me'. Eli said 'I did not call. Go back and lie down'. So he went back and lay down. Once again Yahweh called 'Samuel, Samuel'. Samuel got up and went to Eli and said, 'here I am, since you called me'. He replied 'I did not call you, my son; go back and lie down'.

Samuel had as yet no knowledge of Yahweh, and the Word of Yahweh had not yet been revealed to him. Once again Yahweh called, the third time. He got up and went to Eli and said, 'Here I am, since you called me'. Eli then understood that it was Yahweh who was calling the boy, and he said to Samuel 'Go and lie down, and if someone calls say "Speak, Lord, your servant is listening" '. So Samuel went and lay down in his place. Yahweh then came and stood by, calling as he had done before, 'Samuel, Samuel'. Samuel answered, 'Speak, Lord, your servant is listening'.

• Samuel was clearly someone ready and willing to respond to a call. An attitude of quiet openness is vital, listening to God's silent voice.

• Hear him call you personally, by name, again and again in the silence. God alone knows your real name, your deepest identity and his call is always an invitation to discover your true self.

• God keeps repeating Samuel's name and his call. His call to you is persistent, pressing, persevering. It survives the test of time.

• God's call to Samuel does not come in some extraordinary way. It is hardly recognisable as God's voice at all. God does not come to you in a way that forces your heart. He leaves you free to respond in love.

• We do not always recognise God's voice for what it is, and we can mistake its true meaning. You will need an Eli or two of your own to help you to decipher God's call to you.

• Wait patiently for the Lord, and say to him with your whole being, 'Speak, Lord, your servant is listening.'

Reflection 3: The Call of Mary (Luke 1:26-38)

In the sixth month the angel Gabriel was sent by God to a town in Galilee called Nazareth, to a virgin betrothed to a man named Joseph, of the House of David; and the virgin's name was Mary. He went in and said to her, 'Rejoice, so highly favoured! The Lord is with you.' She was deeply disturbed by these words and asked herself what this greeting could mean, but the angel said to her, 'Mary, do not be afraid; you have won God's favour. Listen! You are to conceive and bear a son, and you must name him Jesus. He will be great and will be called Son of the Most High. The Lord God will give him the throne of his ancestor David; he will rule over the House of Jacob for ever and his reign will have no end.' Mary said to the angel, 'But how can this come about, since I am a virgin?'

'The Holy Spirit will come upon you with its shadow. And so the child will be holy and will be called Son of God. Know this too: your kinswomen Elizabeth has, in her old age, herself conceived a son, and she whom people called barren is now in her sixth month, for nothing is impossible to God.' I am the handmaid of the Lord', said Mary, 'let what you have said be done to me.'

• Together as Christ's Church we share Mary's special calling to be a Christ-bearer, a bringer of the Lord to the world. There can be no greater calling than that.

• Your response to any special calling from God will surely be the same as that of the Virgin Mary. You are disturbed by what God's words to you may mean. You cannot see why God should choose you. 'But how can this come about?' you ask.

• God's first words are always the same: 'Peace', 'Do not be afraid', 'I am with you'.

• If God is calling you to be a priest, or to serve him in some other special way, he will give you whatever strength is needed: 'The Holy Spirit will come upon you, and the power of the Most High will cover you with its shadow'.

• You may feel that, like Elizabeth, your life is too barren to be of use to the Lord, but for you too 'nothing is impossible to God'.

• Your response to God should be the same as Mary's: 'I am the servant of the Lord; let what you have said to be done to me'.

• Ask Our Lady to pray for you. She is the mother of Jesus and of us, his Church. Ask her to pray that God will show you in what special way you are to bear his Son to the world.

Reflection 4: The call of Peter (Luke 5:1-11)

St Peter is someone with whom it is easy to identify. In the Gospels he is a very down-to-earth character. We can see in him our own weaknesses, doubts and hesitations. Peter too was well aware of his unworthiness. Yet he was also a very willing person, with a strong sense of wanting to do God's will.

We see in Peter both the call we all share, the call to follow Jesus, and also the special calling to the pastoral ministry. As you think more deeply about whether Jesus may be calling you to be a priest, it may help to reflect prayerfully on this encounter between Jesus and Simon Peter. Put yourself in Peter's place. Jesus is just as present to you now as he was to Peter then.

> *Now he was standing one day by the Lake of Gennesaret, with the crowd pressing round him listening to the word of God, when he caught sight of two boats close to the bank. The fishermen had gone out of them and were washing their nets. He got into one of the boats – it was Simon's – and asked him to put out a little from the shore. Then he sat down and taught the crowds from the boat.*
>
> *When he had finished speaking he said to Simon 'Put out into deep water and pay out your nets for a catch.' 'Master,' Simon replied, 'we worked hard all night long and caught nothing, but if you say so, I will pay out the nets.' And when they had done this they netted such a huge number of fish that their nets began to tear, so they signalled to their companions in the other boat to come and help them; when these came, they filled the two boats to sinking point.*
>
> *When Simon Peter saw this he fell at the knees of Jesus saying, 'Leave me, Lord; I am a sinful man'. For he and his companions were completely overcome by the catch they had made; so also were James and John, sons of Zebedee, who were Simon's partners. But Jesus said to Simon, "Do not be afraid; from now on it is people you will catch'. Then, bring their boats back to land, they left everything and followed him.*

• Jesus just gets into Simon's boat; he does not ask permission first. It is always he who makes the first move. He comes to you where you are, into your life as it is.

• His presence in your life may work wonders for what you are already doing – your work, your relationships, your service of the Church – but that does not mean he may not be calling you to something else, something which may involve leaving behind what you have and do now.

• Jesus himself is the Fisher of God's People. He casts out the all-embracing nets of his love through the humble fishing of his apostles and those who share their work today.

• Your response to a strong feeling of being called may well be the same as Peter's: 'Leave me, Lord; I am a sinful man'. You may have a sinking feeling, weighed down by what the Lord may be asking of you. But his words to you are the same, too: 'Don't be afraid!'

• Jesus is already in the boat of your life, with you and calling you. Listen to his voice, and seek to say a deeper 'Yes' to whatever he is asking of you. Then with Peter you will be able to say to Jesus, 'If you say so, I will do it'.

Reflection 5: Will you lay down your life for the sheep? (John 10:11-16)

Most people on England and Wales rarely if ever see a shepherd, and yet the image of a shepherd still retains its power today. The priest is ordained to a pastoral or 'shepherding' ministry, making present in the Church the continuing presence of Jesus the Good Shepherd. If you are being called to be a priest, your vocation is to be a shepherd after God's own heart (Jeremiah 3.15). This passage from St John's Gospel sums up well the challenge of being a shepherd of Christ.

I am the good shepherd:
The good shepherd is one
Who lays down his life for his sheep.
The hired man, since he is not the shepherd,
and the sheep do not belong to him,
abandons the sheep and runs away
as soon as he sees a wolf coming,
and then the wolf comes and scatters the sheep;
this is because he is only a hired man
And has no concern for the sheep.
I am the good shepherd;
I know my own and my own know me,
Just as the Father knows me and I know the Father;
and I lay down my life for my sheep.
And there are other sheep I have
That are not of this fold,
and these I have to lead as well.
They too will listen to my voice
and there will be only one flock and one shepherd.

• Jesus is your Shepherd, and the only Shepherd of your parish or chaplaincy. He knows you personally, nourishes you, brings you back when you stray, heals, guides and leads you. He has laid down his life for you.

• Do you have a strong sense of being called to be a good shepherd, not a hired man? Are you ready to lay down your life for the sheep, of your own free will to give your 'all' in service of Jesus and his flock?

• Are you prepared to be a humble sign and instrument of the Good Shepherd? Are you willing to get to know the people, to feed them with God's Word and Sacraments, to be a true pastoral leader, gathering people together around Jesus? Will you abandon your life so fully to God that, through you, he can with a shepherd's crook lead his people to pasture (Micah 7.14)? Read Ezekiel, chapter 34.

• Are you prepared to live out Jesus' words above in your own life here and now?

Suggested Reading List

The Risk of Discipleship: The Catholic Priesthood
by Roderick Strange
Darton, Longman & Todd Ltd (March 2004)

Priesthood in Reality: Living the Vocation of a Diocesan Priest in a Changing World
by Tony Philpot
Kevin Mayhew (December 1997)

A Spiritual Theology of the Priesthood: The Mystery of Christ and the Mission of the Priest
by Dermot A. Power
Continuum International Publishing Group (1998)

Living Priesthood
by Michael Hollings
McCrimmon Publishing Company (1977)

Tears at Night, Joy at Dawn: Journal of a Dying Seminarian
by Andrew Robinson, Michael Conway (Editor)
Alive Publishing Ltd (2003)

The Theology of Priesthood
Goergen, Garrido & Ashley (Editors)
The Liturgical Press (2001)

Ministers of Your Joy
by Cardinal Joseph Ratzinger
St Paul's Publications (1989)

Pastores Dabo Vobis
Pope John Paul II
Catholic Truth Society (1992)

The Joy of Priesthood
by Stephen J Rossetti
Ave Maria Press (2005)

Priest: Portraits of Ten Good Men Serving the Church
by Michael S Rose
Sophia Institute Publications (2003)

In Verbo Tuo
Libreria Editrice Vaticana (1997) - also online at www.vatican.va

Websites

The Catholic Church in England and Wales has an official website for diocesan priesthood. Information about the training, life and ministry of a priest, along with up to date contact information can be found at *www.ukpriest.org*

Statistics

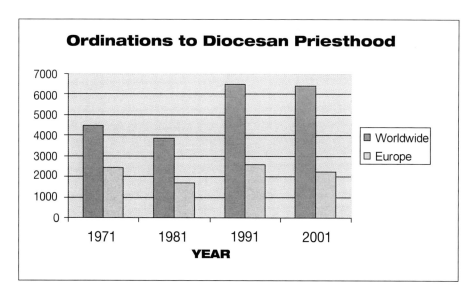

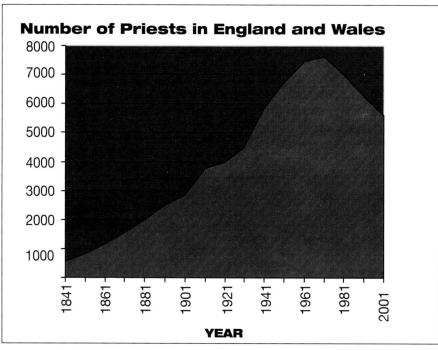